Islam
and the
West

**A New Political and Religious Order
post September 11**

Robert Van de Weyer

BOOKS

Copyright © 2001 0 Books
Text © 2001 Robert Van de Weyer
Cover illustration © 2001 Tamara Beckwith/Rex Features

ISBN 1-903816-14-9

Published in Malaysia for
Synergy Books International
7 Jalan Bangsar Utama 3
Bangsar
59000 Kuala Lumpur
Malaysia

Typography by Jim Weaver Design

Write to:
O Books
John Hunt Publishing Ltd
46A West Street
Alresford
Hampshire SO24 9AU
UK

A CIP catalogue record for this book is available from the British Library.

Printed in Guernsey, Channel Islands

Visit us on the Web at: www.o-books.net

Contents

Part 1: 'Why do they hate us?'
Islam and the West in conflict

Part 2: 'Is mutual respect possible?'
Islam and the West in harmony

Part 3: 'What can we do – politically?'
The politics of peace

Part 4: 'What can we do – religiously?'
The religion of peace

Preface

THIS BOOK has been written in the wake of the events of September 11, 2001. Terrible as they were, those events offer a political and religious opportunity that, if seized, will bring great and lasting benefits across the world – making similar events less and less likely.

I have worked for twenty years as a university lecturer in political economy; and for an equally long period I have been minister of a small church that draws wisdom from all religions. By these two activities the ideas contained in this book have been forged.

Prior to September 11 many of the ideas, both political and religious, would have seemed too radical to merit serious consideration. Yet the attack on the World Trade Center and Pentagon has set off an intellectual earthquake, in which political and religious attitudes are moving with great speed in astonishing and unexpected directions. As a result this book may seem quite moderate.

I am aware that, as a result of my great width of focus, many parts of the picture are shown in insufficient detail. But I have sought to deal with all the major political and religious issues that September 11 raises, and to discern the connections between them. The quality of newspaper and magazine articles focusing on particular issues has been remarkably high; and some articles have also explored the historical background, which is vital for a proper understanding. This book provides an opportunity to stand back and look at the picture as a whole.

It is possible that, by the time this book is published, events may have overtaken a few of the facts mentioned in it. But nothing is likely to alter its central arguments.

Robert Van de Weyer, September 30th, 2001
RobertVandeWeyer@AOL.com

Introduction:
anguished questions

WITHIN HOURS of the planes hurtling into the World Trade Center and the Pentagon on September 11, 2001, Americans were crying out in anguish: 'Why do they hate us?' The question was echoed throughout Europe, since no one doubted that the attack was directed not just at America, but at the whole of western civilization.

It is a terrible question to ask, because it suggests that the West may in some way be responsible, not for the atrocity itself, but for the conditions that motivated it. Yet the nature of the atrocity forces us to ask it. We can tighten our security, we can improve our intelligence, and we can deploy our most sophisticated weaponry. But most military experts tell us that, while such measures may inhibit terrorism, they can never overcome it. And we need only look to the conflicts between Israel and Palestine, between the IRA and Britain, and between ETA and Spain for confirmation of this glum prognosis. The British can cast their minds back into history for further confirmation: in the heyday of their empire, when their military might was unsurpassed, they frequently suffered heavy casualties from Muslim warriors skilled in the use of terror; and on one occasion on the north-west frontier of India over two thousand women and children were slaughtered in a single day, along with almost five thousand soldiers – a death toll similar to that of September 11. The ultimate defeat of Islamic terrorism will only occur when the well of hatred dries up, so smart young Muslims and wealthy older Muslims – modern terrorist warfare requires both great mental ability and substantial funds – can no longer drink from it.

As we stare down that well, we see in its murky waters thirteen centuries of rivalry between Islam and Christianity, between the Muslim world and the western world. Within a century of Islam bursting out of the Arabian peninsula, Arab armies had subdued almost the whole of Christendom, and were only halted in western France. A few centuries later European Christians tried to take their revenge in the Crusades. Soon afterwards Turkish Muslims were forcing their way into Europe, and were halted at Vienna. Then through a combination of capitalism and science western Europe became both rich and powerful; and by the early twentieth century most of the Muslim world was under direct European rule. Today, although every Muslim country is independent, western capitalism and science are more dominant than ever. And just as Baghdad and later Istanbul were the hubs of great Muslim empires, so New York is the symbolic capital of the West. The Islamic crusade against western influence began two centuries ago in the Arabian desert, and Islamic militancy is now entrenched in most Muslim countries. Its primary targets have been the governments of those countries, which the militants regard as too western in both style and policy. But in recent decades some militant groups have begun to turn their crusade of terror towards the West itself. There can be little doubt that, in the eyes of Islamic militants, the destruction of the World Trade Center is no more than an early victory in a long war.

Although enmity between Islam and the West goes back a long way, Muslims are not unique in trying to resist western influence. Chinese resentment of the West flared up in the Boxer rebellion almost a century ago, in which large numbers of westerners were massacred. Gandhi's independence movement in India studiously avoided violence, but was no less determined. And we can find other movements, both bloody and peaceful, throughout Asia and Africa, in which local cultures have reasserted themselves. In recent years the growing movement against globalization has been founded on the conviction that unfettered western capitalism, while making the West richer, has made much of the rest of the world poorer. Thus, while few people anywhere in the world approve the methods of Islamic terrorism, many people everywhere in the world understand the roots of Muslim resentment.

The first question about hatred begs a sequel: 'Is mutual respect possible?' The answer is also to be found in history; and happily it is affirmative. Throughout the past millennium there have been hugely fruitful exchanges between Islam and the West, in the sciences and medicine, in mathematics and astronomy, in the arts and philosophy, and most especially in religion and ethics – including the ethics of war. And both sides have gained in equal measure. Indeed, the European renaissance, in which modern western life was born, would have been impossible without the influence of Islam; while Islam itself would have been impossible without Christianity. Thus we note that in the spheres of politics and economics Islam and the West are often in conflict, whereas in knowledge and ideas they are often in harmony. And we must wonder whether this insight may have wider application: that, while political and economic globalization produces enmity across the world, intellectual globalization brings peace.

Now comes a third question, which is at the crux of our present dilemma: 'What can we do to enable mutual respect overcome hatred?' Even to pose this question is to risk western indignation. Although anti-Islamic feelings lurk in some western hearts, those feelings are surely trivial compared with the terrorists' loathing of the West. So the primary responsibility for overcoming hatred, westerners may reasonably assert, lies within Islam. Yet if westerners have contributed to the conditions nurturing hatred, then westerners must contribute to the task of changing those conditions. And since in the present era the West is dominant, the West is best placed to begin the process of change. Besides, self-protection demands this.

The history of conflict and harmony between Islam and the West suggests that this question must be answered at two levels, the economic and political level, and the religious and moral level. The West is rightly proud of its political freedom. But many in the West wrongly assume that political freedom also implies unfettered economic freedom, in which the market mechanism is supreme – a type of freedom symbolized by the World Trade Center. On the contrary, political freedom, which is based on democracy and the rule of law, implies that the people as a whole have the right and obligation to constrain the actions of individuals if they threaten the common good. This is a truth that Islam has well understood; indeed, the Muslim empires pioneered the notion of strong laws based on political consensus. In the present era global peace depends on the political will to create a legal framework for global capitalism, so that all benefit; it depends on our understanding the true nature of the political freedom that we treasure so highly.

We do not need to know the identities of the hijackers, nor the name of the group to which they belonged, to realize that religion inspired them; only people motivated by the most fervent religious zeal could have gone willingly and deliberately to their own deaths in order to cause the deaths of thousands of others. And the understandable reaction of many westerners is to spit at religion itself, pointing not only to the present carnage, but also to all the wars throughout history fought in the name of some religious creed. Yet human beings are innately religious, in that they wish to exert some degree of control over their inner selves, and use symbols and rituals as means of achieving this. Thus we cannot abolish religion, but must distinguish between good and bad religion – between those religions that nurture love and tolerance in the human psyche, and those that nurture hate and bigotry. Both Islam and Christianity, in common with all the other major religions, have good forms and bad forms; and undoubtedly the form of fundamentalist Islam espoused by terrorists is disgustingly bad. In addition, in an age of global communication and intellectual skepticism, we must find religious forms that are plausible; any kind of fundamentalism, in which some book or set of doctrines is deemed to encapsulate the truth, is wholly implausible. The search for good, plausible religion is ultimately our greatest challenge; it offers our best hope for permanent peace.

'Why do they hate us?' 'Is mutual respect possible?' 'What can we do?' Parts 1 and 2 of this book concern the first and second questions respectively, and parts 3 and 4 concern the third question. Every religion contains the idea of good coming out of bad; and all of us in our personal life have experienced numerous instances of this. Great good may surely come out of the terrible evil of September 11. As we try to answer those three questions, we shall find ourselves addressing other problems, besides terrorism, besetting humanity, some of which pose an even greater threat to humanity's future. And in misty outline we shall discern a new political and religious order. If we start marching towards it, the thousands of victims of September 11 will not have died in vain.

Part 1:

'Why do they hate us?' Islam and the West in conflict

The Arab Empire

MUHAMMAD began to hear words, which he took to be divine revelations, in the year 610; these words were written down to form the Quran, the Islamic holy book. By the time of his death in 632 he had united all the warring tribes of the Arabian peninsula under his leadership, and convinced them of the truth of the Quran. During the following century Arab warriors, inspired by the Quran, created an empire that spread across the Middle East, Iran and Armenia to the borders of Afghanistan, and included the whole of North Africa, Spain and Portugal, and most of central Europe. In 732, exactly a hundred years after Muhammad's death, the western advance of the empire was halted in France at Poitiers. But Islamic imperial power later spread eastwards to the Indian sub-continent; and eventually the whole of central Asia and much of southeast Asia also became Muslim.

The conquering Arabs had little doubt that they were fulfilling a divine plan, and that Allah was guiding them to victory. The peoples and nations subdued by them were mostly Christian; indeed the Arab empire of the eighth century covered with remarkable precision the areas that had embraced Christianity. The Arabs were forbidden by the Quran from compelling Christians to embrace Islam; they merely imposed a heavier tax on them, otherwise allowing them to worship freely. Nonetheless the majority of Christians in North Africa and the Middle East agreed with the Arab interpretation of events, and converted. So the original heartlands of Christendom became Muslim.

But the Christians of Europe, especially western Europe, remained more defiant. The re-conquest of Spain by Christian forces began in the year 1000; and the Muslim rulers in parts of Italy and Sicily were driven out in 1061. In the Christian literature of western Europe Muhammad was vilified as an imposter driven by lust for power and women, and was identified as the anti-Christ. Dante in *The Divine Comedy* consigned Muhammad to the lowest level of hell. The hatred of western Europeans for the Muslim infidel knew few bounds.

The Crusades

MUHAMMAD visited Jerusalem as young man, leading a caravan owned by the woman whom he later married. Jerusalem was the major trading center for goods from the Arabian peninsula, and Muhammad was impressed by its cosmopolitan sophistication and by its religious sites. In particular the ruins of Solomon's temple, the Wailing Wall, imprinted itself on his imagination; and years afterwards he dreamt of ascending a beautiful ladder in the temple, which led up to heaven – where he met Abraham, Moses, Aaron, and two cousins of Jesus. So when after his death the Arabs began their imperial adventures, Jerusalem was an early target; and it fell to them in 638. They then set about building a shrine, the Dome of the Rock, and a mosque, the al-Aqsa, near the Wailing Wall. But they left the churches and the Christian population unmolested; and they permitted the Jews, who had been banned from the city by the Christian rulers, to return.

The loss of Jerusalem was in itself of little consequence to Christians elsewhere, especially as the Muslim conquerors put no restrictions on Christian pilgrims visiting the city. Even in the eleventh century, as confidence amongst Christians in Europe began to return, the political status of Jerusalem remained largely a matter of indifference. However, in 1071 the Christian emperor of Constantinople, whose empire had already been severely curtailed by Arab expansion, suffered a further heavy defeat at the hands of a new Muslim dynasty, the Seljuks, which also took control of Jerusalem at around this time. The emperor now feared for his survival; he was also concerned that the Seljuks would close the pilgrimage route to Jerusalem. So he appealed to the pope in Rome and the Christian rulers of western Europe for support, proposing that they organize a military pilgrimage, with the purpose of protecting the route – and ultimately recapturing the holy city itself.

The pope responded eagerly, calculating that, if he were to organize such a crusade, his own power would be greatly enhanced. The European rulers and nobility saw the possibility of extending their power, especially if they could establish permanent colonies in the Middle East. And European merchants were keen to establish lucrative commercial links. These political and commercial ambitions combined with genuine religious zeal to produce a frenzy of enthusiasm; and the first crusade began. Progress was initially quite slow; but in 1099 the crusaders stormed Jerusalem, and for the first time in almost half a millennium they brought it under Christian sovereignty.

The Christian hatred and resentment of Islam now had free reign. The crusaders systematically slaughtered every Muslim in the city, including women and children; there was not a single survivor. They turned the Dome of the Rock into a church, and converted the al-Asqa mosque into a palace for a Christian king; and they destroyed every other Muslim religious site. Similar massacres and desecrations occurred in other Middle Eastern cities, such as Antioch and Tyre, and in surrounding areas.

Christian rule in Jerusalem lasted less than a century. In 1187 a Muslim commander called Salah al-din – known as Saladin in the West – marched on the city. A story is told that St Francis of Assisi, who loathed the bloodlust of the crusaders, went to Jerusalem, and then calmly walked out of the city to the Muslim encampment, in order to speak to Saladin about Jesus Christ. Saladin received him warmly, and acknowledged him as a worthy witness to Christ's love. But he added that as a religion Christianity must be very feeble, since it had failed to restrain the crusaders' cruelty – while Islam by contrast enabled its adherents to maintain the highest moral standards. Francis had no reply, and returned to Jerusalem with his head bowed. When Saladin and his soldiers captured the city, their magnanimity seemed to prove his words: civilians were spared, and churches and shrines were left untouched.

The Ottoman Empire

AT MUHAMMAD'S death his father-in-law was appointed successor – caliph – to rule the Muslim community. And despite various disputes and schisms, most notably the separation of the Shi'ites in 662, there had been a continuous line of caliphs ruling the Arab empire, initially from Damascus, and then from Baghdad. But by the thirteenth century the empire had largely fragmented into a series of separate states, each ruled by its own sultan who paid the caliph only lip service. In 1258 the empire collapsed completely when a Mongol army, led by a grandson of Genghis Khan, captured Baghdad, burned the city and slaughtered the inhabitants, and executed the caliph and his family. For a few decades Mongol commanders ruled most the Arab territories, although Egypt and Syria successfully resisted Mongol attack.

However, if Islam's enemies now felt more secure, their comfort was short-lived: soon three new Muslim empires arose, and extended Islamic rule far beyond the original Arab dominions. Isfahan became the capital of a great Iranian empire, which spread northwards into central Asia and eastwards to include Afghanistan. Delhi became the capital of the Mughal empire that included most of the Indian subcontinent. And Constantinople, renamed Istanbul, became the center of the Ottoman empire – which soon began the threaten Christian Europe.

By the time Constantinople fell to the Ottomans in 1453, they had already assimilated most of Asia Minor, the area now called Turkey.

Six years later they overran Serbia, and soon afterwards they conquered Bosnia. Early in the following century they incorporated much of Hungary. Their European advance was only halted in 1683 – on September 11 – when their siege of Vienna failed. In the meantime the Ottoman empire spread across north Africa, southern Russia, and Arabia; and Ottoman warships challenged Spain's naval supremacy. Once again Muslims and their religion became objects of the deepest loathing and fear amongst Christians.

The Ottomans, whose ethnic origins remain a matter of dispute, were far more sophisticated in their political methods than the Arabs had been. The Arabs mainly took over the existing political systems of the conquered lands, so that each area of their empire was ruled quite differently; their main concern was to spread Islam and the Arabic language. This political diversity undoubtedly contributed to the Arab empire's eventual collapse. The Ottomans by contrast imposed their own centralized bureaucracy, whose main purpose was to impose and collect extremely heavy taxes. The revenue was then spent partly on military activity, and partly on building some of the most magnificent palaces that the world had seen.

But like the Arab rulers the Ottomans made no attempt to impose Islam by force. Indeed, their main religious concern was to prevent tension between the different religious groups within their empire. To this end they organized a separate judicial system for each religious group that incorporated the group's particular laws and customs. And where members of different groups were living together in a single region, such as Bosnia, separate courts functioned side by side.

Western imperialism

PEOPLE traveling between the Christian and Muslim worlds, at any time between the eighth and the seventeenth centuries, were struck by the comfort and stability enjoyed by most Muslims, compared with the poverty, disease and violence suffered by the majority of Christians. Most caliphs and sultans had a high regard for the law, so in general they ruled fairly and justly; and within the Arab and the Ottoman empires peace prevailed. So individuals could till the soil and ply their trades with little interference, to the benefit of all. Moreover, the Muslim rulers prized every kind of scholarship, especially the sciences; so there was steady progress in technology and medicine. By contrast the kingdoms of Europe were frequently at war with one another; the feudal system of agriculture created little surplus to allow other trades to thrive; and the church was deeply suspicious of any kind of scientific endeavor.

But from the late seventeenth century the relative positions of the two worlds reversed with great rapidity. The Ottoman empire's heavy taxation discouraged enterprise, so the economy stagnated. And the Ottoman bureaucracy became hereditary, employing all the sons of existing officials; so it become both incompetent and bloated – requiring even heavier taxes to maintain. In northern Europe, however, a new class of energetic entrepreneurs arose, financed by bankers and investors who were willing to take considerable risks; and this capitalist spirit soon spread to southern Europe as well. At the same time science broke free from its ecclesiastical shackles, so technology advanced with increasing speed. And the bitter religious battles of the early seventeenth century, between Protestant and Catholic, High Churchman and Puritan, convinced people of the futility of war; so within Europe itself a period of relative peace began, which lasted, with some severe interruptions, for over two centuries.

Even before capitalism had begun to flourish, European sailors had already begun to erode Muslim dominance. Most notably when Vasco da Gama rounded the southern tip of Africa in 1498, and continued onwards to India, he broke the Muslim monopoly of the monsoon trade routes; and by cruel irony his pilot was a great Muslim seafarer, called Ibn Majid. By 1508 the Portuguese were powerful enough to impose restrictions on trade between India and the Gulf. A century later the Portuguese, the Dutch and the British were competing in south-east Asia over the valuable spice trade; and to promote their interests they were each trying to establish colonial rule over Muslim kingdoms in that area.

But these were only the opening skirmishes in a process of economic and political conquest whose extent and effects have far exceeded that of the Arabs and Ottomans combined; and capitalism was the main weapon. In 1603 the East India Company was formed by a group of English merchants; and soon it was forming military alliances with local Indian potentates, many of whom saw personal advantage in breaking away from Mughal rule. By the mid nineteenth century, through the trading networks established by the East India Company, Indian farmers was producing vast amounts of raw cotton for the factories of northern England; and the factory-owners exported the cloth back to India, undercutting the local spinners and weavers who had been central to rural prosperity. The Company was also involved in most other sectors of the Indian economy, remitting vast profits back to Britain. And to protect its commercial interests,

Company officials, protected by a highly efficient army, ruled directly or indirectly almost the entire subcontinent. After the Indian 'mutiny' of 1857 was successfully put down, the last Muhgal emperor was deposed, and the Company was replaced as the ruling power by the British government; soon afterwards Queen Victoria was proclaimed 'Empress of India'

The colonization of India, in which commerce led and politics followed, became a model that all the main European powers followed throughout Asia and Africa, carving up the two continents between them. And since Islam was the dominant religion in much of Asia, almost all of north Africa, and a sizeable portion of sub-Saharan Africa, most Muslims found themselves under European rule. France concentrated on the western end of the Muslim world, occupying Algiers in 1830, and then gradually extending its control over the Sahara. In 1881 it occupied Tunisia; and three decades later the Sultan of Morocco, still nominally independent, sought French support against Muslim insurgents within his own country. Spain, now feeling threatened by French power both to its north and to its south, reacted by occupying a chunk of western Morocco. Britain had already established a protectorate in Egypt, taking it out of Ottoman control; and in 1911 Italy decided to conquer the remaining Ottoman territories to the west of Egypt. The remnants of the Ottoman empire allied with Germany in the First World War; and after Germany's defeat the Ottoman's Muslim territories in the Middle East were divided between Britain and France, with Britain taking Palestine, Jordan and Iraq, and France having Syria and Lebanon. By 1920 the only Muslim countries not under European control were Turkey, Afghanistan, Arabia, northern Yemen, and Iran; and Iran – or Persia, as it was then called – rapidly became a client state of Britain, who wished to protect its expanding oil company there – the forerunner of BP.

Thus the Islamic peoples who had once ruled and converted the heartlands of Christianity, and then at various times colonized large parts of Christian Europe, were now living under European domination.

The European empires of the nineteenth and early twentieth centuries were remarkably similar in their administration to the ancient Islamic empires; and just as Islamic rule had in many respects been benign, so was European rule. The European governments levied taxes on their colonies, and provided political stability and a strong judicial system. They encouraged education and scholarship, establishing schools and colleges. They improved local transport, building roads and railways, which both helped the local economy and enabled their own troops to maintain order more efficiently. They urged charitable organizations to provide hospitals and clinics. And just as the Muslims had made Arabic the common language, so each European power imposed its own language.

In two important respects, however, the European imperialists differed from their Muslim predecessors. First, the Europeans were secular: not only did they allow their subject peoples to practice their own religion, but also they offered no incentive for them to adopt Christianity. They permitted Christian missionary societies to operate in Muslim territories; but they generally gave these societies no official support or blessing. And Muslims were also free to organize their own missionary endeavors, both to resist Christian influence, and to reach more remote groups that professed neither faith. By the nineteenth century most Europeans regarded religion as a matter of personal and private choice that was unconnected with an individual's work or social status; and colonial policy reflected this attitude. As a result in Muslim countries Christian evangelism made virtually no impression – although in the non-Muslim areas of sub-Saharan Africa it was more successful.

Secondly, the Europeans' primary interest was commercial: their troops and administrators provided a secure context for the expansion of European business. This commercialism was quite explicit in the case of the East India Company's colonization of India; and despite pious talk about 'the white man's burden', financial rewards remained the main motive for every colonial venture. Thus, whereas the pattern of daily life remained virtually unchanged in the Muslim empires over many centuries, the economies of the European colonies were transformed within a few decades. Peasant farms producing subsistence crops declined, and large farms and plantations were laid out, producing cash crops for export. Traditional crafts were overwhelmed by imports from European factories; and the surplus labor was employed in the extraction of raw materials for those factories. And while Europeans occupied the highest positions and took the bulk of the profits, local people soon rose to senior posts within European enterprises, and also started their own businesses on western lines. Thus every European colony acquired a local westernized elite; and in Muslim colonies most members of this elite grew away from their old religion, treating it as little more than a picturesque relic of the past.

In the two decades after the Second World War the European empires were disbanded with remarkable speed, and in most cases with little bloodshed. Indeed, in many cases the tax revenues had ceased to cover the growing costs of colonial rule, so the European leaders were happy to grant independence. The reigns of government were quickly taken by the westernized elites; and they in turn were committed to progress on western lines – at an accelerating rate. Thus to devout Muslims, who had watched the influence of their religion rapidly eroding, independence gave cause for even deeper despair; and this despair soon turned to anger.

Islamic militancy

WHEN THE WEST began to assert itself economically and politically over the Muslim world, many Muslims interpreted their material inferiority as an indication that they had been lax in their religion, and hence incurred divine disapproval. In Arabia itself in the mid eighteenth century a theologian called al-Wahhab began a movement to revive the austere simplicity and rigorous discipline of early Islam; and he joined forces with a tribal chief called Muhammad Ibn Saud to drive out the Ottomans, and bring most of the Arabian peninsula into a new Islamic state. The dynasty founded by Ibn Saud is still in power – and hence the state is called Saudi Arabia. Other Muslim reformers urged cautious and gradual modernization in response to the West. In India, for example, Shah Wali Allah hoped to revive the fortunes of the crumbling Mughal empire by persuading Muslims to be more devout. But, rather than wanting slavishly to imitate the ancient past, he advocated the adoption western ideas and practices where they could be reconciled with the Quran.

But western commerce and technology have their own power and momentum that are hard to check. So by the mid nineteenth century it appeared to many Muslims that either they must become wholly westernized, or reject the West altogether; there was no middle way. The outstanding figure urging rejection was a wandering preacher, writer and political activist called al-Afghani. Born in Iran, he stirred up controversy in Afghanistan, Egypt, India, Russia, France, Turkey, and Iran itself. Near the end of his life the Iranian authorities were hunting him down, and they hanged three of his colleagues; but he eluded the noose by dying of cancer. The heart of his message was that Islam is a comprehensive way of life, encompassing worship, law, government and society; so it is utterly incompatible with any kind of western, secular influence. Yet it does not follow that Muslims are condemned to technological backwardness. On the contrary, al-Afghani asserted, science is essentially a Muslim activity, which the West has appropriated; and he pointed to the great Islamic scientists of the medieval period. So he urged Islamic countries simultaneously to reject westernization in public and social life, and at the same time learn western science, in order to carry science forward themselves. Amongst Muslim governments only the Ottomans made a serious attempt to encourage scientific endeavor, inviting westerners to found modern universities on their territory; but, since many of the westerners willing to respond were Christians, hoping to use the universities as means of evangelism, science became associated in people's minds with Christianity – and so was discredited.

In the early decades of the twentieth century the Muslim struggle against the West turned into a mass political movement. In 1928 an Egyptian called al-Banna founded the Muslim Brotherhood, which rapidly spread across the Middle East; and a fellow Egyptian, Sayyid Qutb, supplied its uncompromising ideology. The Brotherhood attracted – and continues to attract – people from all social classes to form 'families', which are brought together into groups; and a number of groups then form a 'battalion'. Members are required to maintain strict personal and moral discipline, and to meet regularly for prayer; athletic training is organized for the young men; and everyone has to engage in a program of Islamic education. Qutb taught that every Muslim government in the Middle East had been corrupted by western ideas, and therefore must be overthrown; governments committed to a rigid application of Islamic law – *sharia*

– should be installed in their place. The Brotherhood's most visible act has been the assassination in 1981 of President Sadat of Egypt, after he had opened Egypt up to western investment. But the Brotherhood now permeates the armed forces and the civil service of most Muslim countries, and has helped to push their governments towards the imposition of the *sharia*. And at every level of society it continues to inflame anti-western emotions.

In western eyes the two most spectacular victories for militant Islam have been the Iranian revolution in 1979, and the capture of Kabul by the Taliban in 1996. The Shah of Iran, and his father before him, tried to westernize their countries, banning Muslim dress in favor of western styles, imposing laws that contradicted the *sharia*, and promoting western forms of education. They also gave generous concessions to western companies who invested in Iran. Whenever the Muslim clergy protested, the Shah reacted with contempt, referring to them as 'black reactionaries'. And he expelled from the country the most vociferous protestor, Ayatollah Khomeini. But in exile Khomeini proved far more dangerous. Aided by modern telecommunications, he rallied support, and meticulously planned the Shah's overthrow; so by the time Khomeini returned in triumph, even the wealthy businessmen welcomed him. And in deposing the Shah, he also hoped to depose all things western, condemning America as 'the great Satan'.

The Taliban was originally a military group, formed in response to the invasion of Afghanistan by the Soviet Union. And as part of the cold war against the Soviet Union, both America and Britain trained Taliban fighters in guerilla warfare, and supplied both arms and money. Since gaining power the Taliban have shown themselves to be even more rigorous than Khomeini in imposing the *sharia* – or rather, their interpretation of it, which many Islamic legal experts, especially in Iran, regard as crude and distorted.

In the meantime there has been a resurgence of the original militant movement, founded by al-Wahhab in Arabia. Although the Saudi dynasty was brought to power by his movement, no one imagines that the pampered princes of modern Arabia have the remotest interest in his teachings. But a new generation of Muslims, some in Arabia itself, see themselves as al-Wahhab's disciples, forming a network of organizations under a variety of names. They include the Algerian terrorists who have killed tens of thousands of their compatriots in trying to bring down the Algerian government; the Egyptian terrorists who in 1997 killed seventy tourists in Luxor; the Kashmiri terrorists who kill innocent Hindus and western travelers in striving to gain independence from India; and, above all, Osama bin Laden and his al-Qaida group. Al-Wahhab himself authorized terrorist acts in his campaign to take over Arabia; for example, in 1801 the Wahhabis slaughtered two thousand ordinary citizens in the streets of Qarbala. His modern followers have long surpassed his grisly record.

While the relative poverty of the Middle East in relation to the West has been the spur to militancy, it is not poverty itself that drives individuals to become militants. On the contrary, most of the leading militants are from relatively wealthy families, and many have even received western-style education. For them the Middle East's economic problems are a source of humiliation, and thence an affront to their faith; and their knowledge of the West serves to deepen this inner wound. Waging war on the West is a means of restoring their self-respect.

Zionism

IN MUHAMMAD'S time there were groups of Jews in the major Arabian cities, mostly engaged in trade. Muhammad acquainted himself with their religion, which he held in very high regard. And when he received the words of the Quran, he saw himself as another prophet on the Jewish model – a spiritual descendant of Abraham, Moses, Elijah, Isaiah and the rest. Thus he expected the Jews of Arabia to support him in his quest to call the Arabian people to faith in God. But, according to the authoritative accounts of Muhammad's life, the Arabian Jews refused to accept him as a prophet, and they mocked his religious teaching as crude and naïve. Despite his deep disappointment he refused to condemn or persecute them, and his belief in the fundamental unity of Islam and Judaism was undimmed. This tolerant and respectful attitude towards Jews and their faith remained the norm amongst Muslims for thirteen centuries; it was Christians, not Muslims, who acquired the stain of Jewish blood on their hands.

But with the rise of Zionism in the twentieth century, rooted in a western interpretation of Judaism, and supported by western money and weapons, tolerance turned into hatred and respect into contempt. And as we enter the twenty-first century, Zionism is a central focus of Muslim enmity towards the West.

The origins of Zionism lie in a strange combination of German nationalism, Jewish prosperity, Christian zeal, and anti-Semitism. Through the nineteenth century, as western Europe societies became more secular in outlook, so Jews were assimilated, ceasing to form separate groups; and many rose to great prominence in commerce, politics, the arts and the sciences. Some, like the fathers of the British prime minister Benjamin Disraeli and the social philosopher Karl Marx, abandoned the Jewish faith altogether, and for largely social reasons received Christian baptism. Others remained loyal to Judaism, regarding it as a purely spiritual bond that was entirely compatible with patriotism towards their country. Nowhere was the assimilation more complete than in Germany. Yet the unification of Germany helped to stimulate a fervent sense of German nationhood, and, in the minds of some, a sense of German racial superiority. This had a double effect on German Jews. On the one hand it awakened in them a sense of their own distinct national and racial identity; on the other, it made them feel uncomfortable and unwelcome within Germany.

The success of Jews within western societies, and especially their scientific and artistic eminence, also reawakened their view of themselves as a messianic people, called by God to be a sign of social justice, universal prosperity and permanent peace. And the messianic vision could only be realized within the Jews' historic home: Jews must return in large numbers to Palestine, and create a perfect society in accordance with the Law and the Prophets. As Moses Hess wrote in 1862 in a book provocatively entitled *Rome and Jerusalem*: 'It is only with a national rebirth that the religious genius of the Jews, like the giant of the legend touching Mother Earth, will be endowed with new strength and again be inspired with the prophetic spirit.' Not only did many of Hess's fellow Jews respond with enthusiasm; but so also did a small, but influential, number of Christians. The Earl of Shaftesbury in England, renowned as a social reformer and the leader of the Evangelical movement within the Church of England, regarded the return of Jews to Palestine as the fulfillment of prophecies within the New Testament. He was the first of numerous Evangelical Christians, in Britain and America, to give their fervent support to the Zionist cause.

Initially Jews advocating a return to Palestine envisaged a cluster of agricultural settlements, with some adjoining workshops in which ancient crafts would be practiced; and they also imagined a few cultural and religious centers to which Jews and Gentiles from across the world could visit for inspiration. From the 1870s small groups of Jews from western Europe and Russia began purchasing land from Palestinians, with money from both Jewish and Christian benefactors. And in 1883 the hugely wealthy Jewish banker, Baron Edmond de Rothschild of Paris, began pumping much larger amounts into the establishment of these Jewish colonies. However, this essentially religious movement turned political through the tireless advocacy of an Austrian journalist called Theodor Herzl. By the 1890s German and Austrian nationalism was starting to express itself in strong antipathy to Jews and to the economic privileges they had won for themselves; and the Dreyfus affair in France showed that anti-Semitism was spreading. Herzl concluded that permanent assimilation of Jews into European life was impossible; and in 1896 he published a pamphlet entitled *The Jewish State*, in which he proposed forming a new Jewish nation in Palestine. In a novel published six years later he depicted this nation as a kind of Jewish version of a western European state, a Hebrew Vienna. A follower of Herzl coined the name 'Zionism' for Herzl's vision – Zion being the hill in Jerusalem where King Solomon built the temple.

In the early years of the twentieth century the flow of Jews to Palestine increased rapidly, so that by 1914 there were about 90,000; and the flow of money from wealthy Jews remaining in Europe rose in proportion. In 1917 the leaders of the Zionist movement achieved their first major political victory: they persuaded the British government publicly to declare its support for 'the establishment in Palestine of a national home for the Jewish people.' The only Jew in the British cabinet was opposed to this declaration, expressing the fear that involving Judaism in politics would corrupt its spiritual purity, compromise its message, and, worst of all, be a further spur to anti-Semitism. And his unease about Zionism was now felt by a growing number of European Jews. But his Christian colleagues overruled him.

When in the aftermath of the First World War Britain took control of Palestine, Zionist hopes rose. British policy in Palestine, however, was confused. To enable the establishment of a Jewish national home the British authorities encouraged Jewish immigration, so within a decade the Jewish population in Palestine tripled; and the area of Palestine owned by Jews also multiplied. The authorities also allowed the Jews to build an entire city, Tel Aviv, as the center of Jewish industry and commerce. But the declaration of 1917 – known as the Balfour Declaration, after the devoutly Christian foreign secretary who wrote it – deliberately stopped short of advocating a Jewish state; and it contained the proviso that 'nothing shall be done which may prejudice the civil and religious rights of existing non-Jewish communities in Palestine.' So the British authorities strived to ensure peaceful co-existence between the Muslim Palestinians and the Jewish settlers, hoping that in due course the two groups would come together to form a single independent state. Indeed, peaceful co-existence had also been Herzl's dream.

But it soon became clear that a Jewish national home and the upholding of Palestinian rights were incompatible – as wise heads had predicted. And the British found themselves caught between Jew and Arab, taking the brunt of both sides' anger. The Palestinian Arabs feared that a Jewish state, in which they would be second-class citizens, was the inevitable consequence of unrestricted Jewish immigration; and several times after 1929 they organized revolts, which the British suppressed. Eventually in 1939 the British government acknowledged Palestinian grievances by limiting Jewish immigration to 15,000 people per year. Militant Jews responded by mounting a terrorist campaign against the British, culminating in the bombing in 1946 of the King David Hotel in Jerusalem, which contained British administrative and military offices; ninety-one people were killed. They also organized illegal immigration.

Hitler, through his efforts to exterminate the Jews in Europe, ensured their success in Palestine. Such was the horror and the guilt felt by Europeans at the Holocaust, as the full extent of it became clear, that the British and other European governments no longer felt able to resist Jewish demands. Besides, Jewish terrorism had worn down British resolve. So in 1948 the British withdrew, and the state of Israel was proclaimed.

The legacy

IMPERIAL RULERS may treat their subjects with tolerance and even kindness. The Muslim empires stretching into Europe in medieval times were commendably tolerant towards both Christians and Jews, and were occasionally benevolent. The European empires of the recent past, stretching across the historic lands of Islam, were also tolerant; and many European governors and administrators, often motivated by Christian faith, made great efforts to improve the lives of their subjects. But when people of one culture and religion rule by force those of a different culture and religion, there is inevitably a legacy of deep bitterness. The appalling cruelty of the crusaders towards innocent Muslims was one expression of such bitterness; the appalling cruelty of Islamic terrorists towards westerners is another expression. Neither is excusable, but both are understandable.

The additional and crucial twist for Muslims is that, while the western empires have been dismantled, western dominance persists and grows. When the Arabs, and later the Ottomans, withdrew from Christian Europe, they played no further part in European life; so the bitterness could gradually lessen, and Europe's memory of the economic and cultural superiority of Islam could fade. But, since the Muslim countries gained their political freedom, western goods, western investment, and the western media have actually become more, not less, important. Muslims are reminded day by day, hour by hour, of their economic inferiority to, and dependence on, the West. They watch and enjoy Hollywood movies, and admire and envy the

American way of life portrayed in them; but they resent their own inability to provide such a way of life for themselves.

The strength of Zionism both symbolizes and accentuates the Muslim dilemma. Israel is an astonishing economic success: it has made deserts bloom, created thriving industries from nothing, and in recent years has been amongst the leaders in technological innovation. And with American arms it has formed an army that on three occasions has defeated the combined forces of its Arab neighbors, extending its borders in the process. In Arab eyes it is a chunk of the West, in all its material glory, transplanted in their territory – which is precisely how the early Zionists envisaged it. Every Arab sympathizes with the plight of the Palestinians, confined to a small segment of their former homeland; in a recent poll over 60% of the people of Saudi Arabia, Kuwait, the Emirates and Lebanon, and almost 80% of Egyptians, answered that Palestine is 'the single most important issue to them personally.' But the hatred of Zionism is also a proxy for Arab emotions towards the entire western world – and especially America.

Yet Israel is a profoundly flawed symbol of the West; and its flaw causes Muslims, to some degree, to misunderstand the West, adding to their resentment. The founding fathers of the United States were passionately secular; they wanted a clear separation between politics and religion, and enshrined this in the Constitution. The nations of western Europe have almost become secular, although a few, like Britain, retain nominal Christian links. Indeed, in the days following September 11 both President Bush in America and Prime Minister Blair in Britain emphasized that the West is not at war with Islam as such, and urged their people to treat their Muslim compatriots with respect. The state of Israel, by contrast, is founded on a particular religion, Judaism, and seeks to embody its religion's values; and it continues to receive financial aid and moral approval from Jews in

America and western Europe, and also from a certain type of Evangelical Christian. Indeed this combination of Jewish and Christian devotion to Israel has virtually compelled American governments to continue supplying weaponry to the Israeli army. Thus for many Arabs the existence of Israel gives their resentment of the West a more pronounced, and largely unjustified, religious dimension.

Through the twentieth century Islamic militancy was mainly directed towards the governments of Muslim countries for adopting policies influenced by western ideas. At the start of the twenty-first century Islamic militancy is turning towards the sources and promoters of those ideas.

Part 2:

'Is mutual love and respect possible?' Islam and the West in harmony

Christian roots of Islam

O N HIS JOURNEY to Jerusalem, leading his future wife's caravan, Muhammad stopped in the shade of a tree that happened to be near the cell of a Christian monk. The monk emerged from his cell, and engaged Muhammad in conversation. The monk was deeply impressed by the young Muhammad's natural wisdom, and prophesied that he would be a messenger of God. Some time later, at Muhammad's wedding, Muhammad's assistant recalled this incident to one of Muhammad's cousins, who was a Christian renowned for the depth of his scholarship. The Christian scholar was inclined to believe the monk's prophecy; he added that he had become weary of waiting for God's messenger, and was now greatly relieved that he had arrived.

These incidents are recalled in a book compiled a few decades after Muhammad's death by a historian called Ibn Ishaq; he collected oral and written accounts of Muhammad's life, and arranged them in chronological order. The incidents convey the importance of Christianity in Muhammad's religious formation. By Muhammad's time Christian monasticism was at its height, and there were tens of thousands of hermits, and many hundreds of monastic communities, scattered across the deserts of the Middle East. Amongst these Christian ascetics many were recognized as prophets, enjoying direct communication with God; and in the surviving monastic literature of this period God frequently speaks. Thus when Muhammad went out night after night into the hills north of Mecca, he would not have been surprised to hear those divine utterances that he later dictated to a scribe,

29

and formed the Quran. And, since Muhammad in his youth relished conversations about religion, it is reasonable to suppose that he had many long discussions about Christianity with his Christian cousin.

In the Quran itself the birth and miracles of Jesus are recounted, and he is acknowledged as a great prophet. And there are many ideas that were current in the Christian theology of Muhammad's time. In particular, the Quran speaks of a day of resurrection in which the dead will be brought back to life; and it emphasizes time and again that this resurrection will be bodily, with people emerging from their graves. At this moment God will pass judgment, casting the wicked into a fiery hell, and directing the righteous to eternal paradise. The Quran denies the divinity of Jesus, saying that all prophets are human beings whom God has chosen; and it denies that the crucifixion ever occurred, hence refuting any notion of the death of Jesus being a sacrifice for human sin. But there were many Christians in Muhammad's time, Arians and Gnostics respectively, who also denied these things – and whom other Christians condemned as heretics. Thus the theology of the Quran may be regarded as a heretical form of Christianity; so Muslims are those who treat the Arian and Gnostic heresies as orthodoxy.

A further incident in the early history of Islam reveals the degree to which Muslims respected and trusted Christians, and the initial unity between them. The Muslim community initially faced vicious opposition from the tribal leaders in Mecca, including several attempts to murder Muhammad himself. Although Muhammad himself remained in Mecca, he sent some of his followers to Ethiopia, a Christian country, for protection. The Ethiopian king received them warmly, and invited them to his court to speak about Muhammad and his message to himself. The king, and the Christian bishops who were in attendance, were deeply impressed by what they heard, and declared that Muhammad was indeed a divine messenger.

Philosophy and theology

I N 641 the Arabs conquered Alexandria. Several centuries earlier this beautiful city on the Egyptian coast had taken over from Athens as the main center of philosophical thought; numerous academies had been founded there, in which the style of intellectual inquiry pioneered by Plato and Aristotle was continued with untiring vigor. And from the third century onwards it had also become a major center of Christian theology; men such as Origen and Clement, who combined fierce intelligence with mystical insight, used the ideas of Plato in particular to develop a Christian understanding of humanity's relationship with divinity. Thus less than a decade after Muhammad's death, his followers – mostly illiterate warriors from the remote Arabian desert – were breathing the air of one of the most sophisticated cultures that the world had seen.

They were invigorated by it. When the Arabs established their capital in Baghdad, the caliph immediately invited philosophers from throughout his empire to join him there; and he built houses for them, and halls in which they could give lectures and hold debates. Some of these philosophers subscribed to no religion, but many were Christian, and some were Jewish; anyone of intellectual ability and deep scholarship was welcome. The caliph's recruitment campaign was helped by the decision of the Christian emperor in Constantinople to banish all philosophers from his empire, even Christian ones, on the grounds that philosophical discussion is

incompatible with Christian belief. This exile occurred in the middle
of the sixth century, and most of the philosophers took refuge in Iran,
where the king was sympathetic. As Iran was absorbed into the Arab
empire, the intellectual descendents of these refugees eagerly moved
to Baghdad.

The first task was to establish communication between the
philosophers, since they spoke and wrote in a variety of different
languages; and naturally the caliph ordered that Arabic should be the
common language. Thus not only did the philosophers themselves
have to master Arabic, but also every philosophical work of merit
had to be translated into Arabic. Thus through the eighth century
many of the great texts of Greek philosophy, including those of
Aristotle and Plato, plus several works in Syriac, were rendered into
the language of the Quran. And, so broad were the intellectual
interests of the Arab rulers, that at least one Hindu work, composed
in Sanskrit, was also translated.

Islamic philosophy now entered a golden age; and in due course
the writings of its leading philosophers were to exert a global
influence, most especially in Christian Europe. Four philosophers
stand out. The first was al-Razi, who was born in about 865. He
trained in medicine, and for much of his life worked as a physician
and hospital administrator. But he wrote at least two philosophical
works, one on ethics entitled *Spiritual Medicine*, and the other,
Philosophic Life, on the relationship between religion and philosophy.
While acknowledging the importance of prophets like Muhammad,
he believed that all religious and ethical truth can be directly attained
by the human mind through rational contemplation. In order to
engage in such contemplation the mind must free itself from all
passion and emotion, and thus become utterly objective; and he
recommended that individuals desiring emotional liberation should
have a personal teacher to guide them. The essence of truth, so the

mind finally discerns, is pure love, whose outward expression is 'to treat all people justly.' Al-Razi condemned all kinds of religious groups whose laws require them to behave unjustly, or to behave justly only towards other members of their group; pure love is universal.

Ibn Sina – known in the West as Avicenna – lived about a century later. He grappled with three theological issues that have dogged Islam and Christianity equally. The first is the existence of evil. He argued that, as creator of the world, God must be responsible for the evil within it: 'If only pure righteousness prevailed in the world, it would be a different world from the one God made.' This led him to the second issue, the notion of reward and punishment. He argued that God has inserted in the human soul a tendency towards goodness, in that good acts bring peace to the soul, whereas bad acts bring turmoil. These inner feelings experienced during earthly life, rather than heaven or hell after death, are the true consequences of our moral choices. And this led to the third issue, the nature of religious language. He acknowledged that prophets have to use stark and simple images in order to convey their message to the common people; but the reflective person should regard these as images and metaphors of the truth, rather than the truth itself. Amongst these metaphors he included not only heaven and hell, but also resurrection and prayer. The resurrection of the body, taught by the Quran, indicates that life continues beyond death; but in fact only the soul survives – a notion that, in Avicenna's eyes, is too subtle for most human beings to comprehend. Praising God and making requests, which are the outward forms of prayer, are really vehicles enabling individuals to align their wills with that of God.

In the early part of his life al-Ghazali, who lived in the eleventh century, put forward a vigorous defense of a literal interpretation of the Quran, giving reasons for believing in the bodily resurrection and in heaven and hell. He also argued that if philosophers pursue reason alone as the means of ascertaining the truth, they must ultimately destroy religion and morality. But according to his autobiography, he gradually grew weary of both philosophy and theology, since they are merely verbal discussions about God. Instead he longed to encounter God face to face. So after much hesitation he decided to train as a mystic: he gave away his wealth, went to live in solitude, and devoted himself to meditation. After ten years he achieved his goal, and experienced a state of certainty and ecstasy. Al-Ghazali's spiritual journey was echoed two centuries later in Paris by Thomas Aquinas, the greatest Christian theologian of medieval times who was deeply influenced by Islamic thought. Towards the end of his life he too had a mystical experience, after which he wrote: 'Such things have been revealed to me that all I have written seems like straw.'

Ibn Rushd, known in the West as Averroes, was born in Cordoba in Spain 1126, and became a judge in his home city; then the sultan of Morocco invited him to be his physician and personal adviser. Whereas al-Razi and Avicenna took their inspiration from Plato, Averroes was a follower of Aristotle, writing a masterly commentary on his works. Like Francis Bacon half a millennium later, Averroes argued that scientific inquiry should be free from religious dogma, since science is essentially a religious activity: by studying creation as it is, the scientist is uncovering the mind of the creator. Like many modern western theologians, he argued that there are many sources of religious insight – natural beauty, dialectical argument, poetry and literature – and that all are equally valid. And like many medieval Christian writers, such as Bernard of Clairvaux, he believed that Scriptures must often be interpreted allegorically.

Throughout the early medieval period – the so-called 'Dark Ages' – there was little interest amongst Christian Europeans in philosophical matters; and the old Latin translations of Plato,

Aristotle and the other ancient Greek philosophers were lost. But by the twelfth century universities were beginning to flourish in a few European cities; and the proximity of Muslim Spain stimulated more adventurous Christian scholars to learn Arabic, and thereby acquaint themselves with Islamic ideas. And as they studied the Muslim philosophers, they were led to the Greek sources that inspired them. Thus Michael the Scot and Herman the German led the way in translating the works of Plato and Aristotle from Arabic into medieval Latin. They also translated the works of the leading Muslim philosophers themselves, in particular Avicenna and Averroes. The effect on European thought was startling. Christian theology burst into life, with theologians re-working the whole of Christian doctrine in the light of Greek philosophy. In his monumental *Summa Theologiae* Thomas Aquinas in the thirteenth century founded his method of argument on Aristotle's system of logic, and his theology itself on Aristotle's philosophical categories and concepts. Aquinas quarreled with Averroes's interpretation of Aristotle's ideas; and in the university of Paris, of which Aquinas was a member, theologians divided into the so-called Latin Averroists and those who followed Aquinas' line. The conflict between the two groups became so fierce that the bishop of Paris eventually had to intervene, coming down on Aquinas' side. The Aristotelian theology of Thomas Aquinas remains the basis of Roman Catholic orthodoxy; and even today men training for the Catholic priesthood have to study his writings.

In due course Europeans made translations of Plato and Aristotle directly from the original Greek; and by the sixteenth century few European writers referred by name to Avicenna and Averroes. But no historian of ideas disputes the continuing indirect influence of these great Muslim philosophers. Indeed, even when the Protestant reformers tried to turn their backs on philosophy itself – Luther referred to is as 'vanity and perdition' – their own styles of argument and even their ideas owe an unconscious debt to Islam. The Protestant elevation of the Bible into the 'word of God' is almost identical to al-Ghazali's understanding of the Quran. And subsequent debates in Protestant churches about biblical interpretation, with those favoring a literal approach opposed by those who see many biblical stories as metaphors and myths, echo Muslim debates about how the words of the Quran should be understood. In the longer run the more profound Muslim influence on European thought was in liberating it from religious dogma. For Avicenna and Averroes spiritual devotion and intellectual inquiry, far from being opposed, complemented one another; indeed, for Averroes unrestrained scientific investigation was actually a religious obligation. The European renaissance, and all that flowed from it, would have been impossible without the winds of freedom that blew from the world of Islam.

Science, mathematics and medicine

N 1575 the Ottoman emperor set up an observatory in Istanbul; and a painting survives of its operation. Every kind of scientific instrument is visible: set squares and protractors, a theodolite and an astrolabe, a spirit level and a clock, a weighing machine using springs and an optical device that appears like a microscope; there is also a globe whose depiction of the continents seems quite accurate. It was at least a century before Europe had anything to match this remarkable establishment; and without the pioneering work of Muslim scientists and mathematicians, the scientific revolution in Europe would have taken far longer.

The painting of the Istanbul observatory illustrates a wider point: that science was integral to the social and political ideology of the Islamic empires. The caliphs in Baghdad believed that their empire incorporated most of the civilized world – they were unaware of how vibrant was the civilization of China. And they saw Islam as the inheritor and guardian of all human knowledge, including mathematics and the natural sciences, with a divine responsibility to push forward the frontiers of knowledge. To fulfill this responsibility they arranged for scientific works from every region of the empire, and beyond, to be translated into Arabic, just as they had organized the translation of philosophical works. Scholars familiar with Greek and Latin, Persian, Syriac and Sanskrit, were recruited for this task – the most famous of these translators, fluent in at least three languages, being a Christian called Hunayn. They also encouraged young men of scientific inclination to do fresh research and write new works, providing whatever facilities they required.

As in ancient Greece, the greatest field of scientific interest was astronomy. As early as 830 Muslim astronomers had produced comprehensive tables for the movements of the sun, the moon and the planets, using mathematical calculations derived from both Indian and Greek sources. But soon these calculations were shown to be flawed, so new methods of calculation had to be found. This led to the development of trigonometry and various other mathematical tools. The most distinguished Islamic astronomer, Ibn al-Shatir, who lived in the fourteenth century, produced a series of mathematical models that were reproduced a century and a half later by Copernicus; and there is reason to think that al-Shatir concluded from these models, as Copernicus did, that the earth was not stationary, but moved round the sun.

Within the sphere of mathematics itself the Muslims adopted the Indian counting system, with the base ten; and they adapted the Indian numerals, enabling any number to be denoted using only nine digits and zero. When many centuries later Europe began using these numerals in place of the cumbersome Roman letters, Europeans had the grace to acknowledge their debt by referring to them as 'Arabic numerals'. In the early ninth century a Muslim genius called al-Khwarizmi invented an entirely new mathematical discipline, algebra; and he showed how algebraic equations, both linear and quadratic, provide an abstract means of solving a wide range of practical problems. A few decades later other mathematicians were demonstrating how algebra may be applied to the branch of mathematics in which the ancient Greeks had excelled, geometry, even suggesting that geometry should be subsumed within algebra. Century after century further new mathematical concepts were developed, including negative and real numbers, decimal fractions, and general algorithms in the theory of equations. In the eleventh century a mathematician called al-Haytham wrote a book applying many of these concepts to optics, which found its way into Europe; it become the standard work on the subject until the seventeenth century. A later Muslim expert in optics, Farisi, explained the rainbow.

Muslim engineers concentrated their main efforts on the extraction, use and distribution of water. They built underground conduits to carry water from aquifers to centers of population, thereby minimizing loss through evaporation. They built dams both for irrigation and for providing waterpower with which to drive mills. They invented complex water-raising machines to place over wells. And they built elegant bridges with water mills attached to their piers. They also worked with architects and artists to create mosques and palaces of breath-taking elegance and beauty.

Muslim physicians had the benefit of Arab translations of both ancient Greek texts, such as the works of Hippocrates, and Indian texts describing the Ayurvedic system; and many of their remedies were derived directly from these sources. However, al-Razi and Avicenna respectively made two advances in medical methodology that laid the foundations for modern western medicine. Al-Razi ran a hospital in which he pioneered experimental research. To test each remedy he divided his patients into two groups, one of which received the remedy, and the other of which did not; he then observed and tabulated the results. The most famous work emerging from these experiments was a monograph on the treatment of smallpox and measles, which guided physicians in Europe right up until the eighteenth century. Avicenna, prompted by Aristotle's work on the subject, realized that a proper understanding of human anatomy is vital in the development of new treatments; and he made the first systematic study of the human body.

Politics and law

WHEN PEOPLE speak of the principles on which western political systems rest, they typically mention democracy and the rule of law. Democracy, in the words of Abraham Lincoln, ensures that government is 'of the people, by the people, and for the people.' The rule of law enables people to know clearly their obligations to society, and the sanctions they will incur if they fail to fulfill those obligations. Together democracy and rule of the law save people from the arbitrary whims of dictators and tyrants, and make all people politically equal. Democracy was pioneered by ancient Athens; the rule of law is to a great degree a product of Islam.

From the outset Islam was a political religion: Muhammad was not only a prophet, but also a charismatic political leader; and when he died, the caliphs succeeding him took over his political – but not his prophetic – role. At first the caliphs, assisted by advisors, made decisions as new problems and issues arose; and they appointed judges to enforce their decisions and to settle disputes. But, while people had trusted that Muhammad's decisions were divinely guided, they had less trust in the caliphs. And as the Muslim territories expanded, absorbing places with quite different customs and traditions from those of the Arabian peninsula, judges were uncertain as to what extent local traditions should influence their rulings. It soon became clear that a unified body of laws was required that would guide – and constrain – both the caliphs and the judges. By the eighth century, in several of the major cities of the empire, there were legal scholars striving to formulate an Islamic legal code; and by the year 900 a highly sophisticated system of law, known as the *sharia*, was in place throughout the Muslim world.

According to al-Shafii, a scholar from Mecca who is commonly recognized as the father of Islamic jurisprudence, the law should have four roots. The first is divine revelation in the Quran. The Quran condemns particular practices, such as murder, theft, usury (charging interest on loans), exploitation of the poor, false contracts, and adultery; and, according to al-Shafii, these practices should be illegal. It also strongly advises against certain forms of behavior, such as drinking alcohol and gambling; and this advice should also be enshrined in law. In addition it indicates a certain ethical bias. For example, while not banning slavery, it urges slave owners to free their slave; while not banning polygamy, it orders men to limit the number of their wives to four; and while permitting divorce, it indicates a strong preference for lifelong unions. Al-Shafii's writings, and those of later jurists following his lead, show how these ethical biases can be applied in law with subtlety and discretion, putting such a price on slavery and polygamy that they disappear of their own accord.

The second root is the *sunna*, the words and deeds of Muhammad. Although, according to the Quran itself, Muhammad was a fallible human being, God chose him as a prophet for his wisdom and insight; so his recorded sayings and his personal example indicate how human beings should live. The *sunna* in turn revealed the third root of law. Muhammad said: 'My community will never agree on an error.' Al-Shafii interpreted this as meaning that, when a general consensus forms that some particular type of behavior is right or wrong, this consensus should be legally binding on individuals. The fourth root is analogical reasoning from the other three roots: some anti-social action, which is not included in the other three roots, may be deemed illegal if it is similar in essence to actions that are included.

Although the Quran is the primary source of Islamic law, legal scholars have always recognized that legal matters comprise only a small portion of it; the main themes of the Quran are basic religious and moral principles. They have also recognized that the teachings of the Quran were in certain parts connected with the particular circumstances of the time and place in which they were revealed. Indeed, the Quran was given to Muhammad gradually over twenty-three years, and some of its contents are explicit responses to events that occurred during that period. Thus from al-Shafii onwards, legal scholars have sought to distill from the Quran the ethical rules that are immutable, and should therefore form the overriding objectives of the *sharia*; and they have allowed for the possibility that the means of fulfilling these objectives may evolve according to changing needs and experience. The overriding objectives are generally held to be the promotion of fairness, equality, prosperity and human dignity, the establishment and maintenance of government that consults the people, the prevention of injury, the removal of hardship, and moral education. An example of the evolution of the *sharia* concerns the treatment of teachers: originally religious teachers were banned from charging fees, as teaching was regarded as an act of spiritual merit; but when too few people offered themselves for this task, modest fees were permitted.

In the heyday of Islamic power, the *sharia* was regarded by Muslims as one of the chief blessings of their religion, and it was the envy of those from outside who visited Muslim lands. But in recent decades, as independent Muslim states have tried to re-impose the *sharia*, virtually all outsiders, and most ordinary Muslims, have been horrified. The problem is that many Muslim politicians and activists today appear ignorant of the third and fourth of al-Shafii's roots. Thus, for example, the Taliban in Afghanistan have formulated a legal code that claims to be based on the Quran and the sayings of

Muhammad, without reference to popular consensus or to rational argument. Al-Shafii well understood that the Quran and the *sunna* are open to widely varying interpretations, and hence consensus and reason are necessary to ensure that interpretations are wise and humane. The Taliban have demonstrated that, when consensus and reason are abandoned, the overriding objectives of the *sharia*, far from being fulfilled, are cruelly frustrated.

Warfare

WHEN MUHAMMAD began his prophetic mission, he saw himself only as a teacher, passing on to his compatriots what God had told him. Then, as the leaders of his own tribe turned against him and his followers, making several attempts on his life, it became clear that Islam would only survive by means of military victory. Ibn Ishaq's biography of Muhammad records the moment when God gave Muhammad permission to call his followers to arms. Until that moment God had required Muhammad 'to endure all the insults thrown at him, and to forgive the ignorance of those who rejected his call, ... while the tribal leaders were free to persecute Muslims without fear of retribution.' From the outset Muhammad had taught his followers that Islam involved a spiritual *jihad* in which they must wage war on the evil inclinations within themselves; now they were free to wage a physical *jihad* against those who uphold evil in the world.

But this divine permission was not without stringent conditions. 'First,' according to Ibn Ishaq's account, 'God ordered Muslims to fight only those who persecuted them for their faith; they should not make war for the sake of gaining power and wealth. Secondly, they should never use deceit in conducting warfare, but should fight honestly. God also commanded that, when they achieve victory, Muslims should not exploit those whom they have vanquished; their only aims should be to enable Islam to be practiced fully and freely, and to ensure that people live in peace with one another.' In his subsequent battles, of which there were several, Muhammad and his followers abided by these conditions strictly. And the conditions passed into the *sharia*, along with two others: that children, women and the elderly shall not be harmed in war; nor should animals, crops and buildings.

Two centuries earlier the north African theologian, Augustine of Hippo, formulated a Christian doctrine of the just war. He argued that Christians should generally use non-violent methods to resolve conflicts, but that violent aggressors may be resisted by violent means. In particular, Christians may use military force to defend their own communities, to protect the innocent and the weak, and to put right monstrous injustices. Later theologians, such as Thomas Aquinas, added further criteria. Only governments with legitimate authority may wage war, not powerful individuals or groups. War should be a last resort, waged only when every attempt at peaceful settlement has failed. A government authorizing war should acknowledge the extent to which the enemy has justice on its side, and in the event of victory should uphold the enemy's rights. An attempt should be made to compare the suffering of war with the suffering that war is intended to alleviate; and war should only be waged if the former is likely to be less than the latter. Injury to non-combatants, including soldiers that are injured or have surrendered, should be avoided. Revenge should never be a motive for war, nor should the acquisition of wealth or power. And finally there should be a reasonable probability of success.

It is highly unlikely that Muhammad had even heard of Augustine of Hippo, let alone been aware of his importance. But, since tribal warfare was a perennial feature of Arab society at that time, it seems likely that he had discussed the ethics of war with Christian acquaintances, including his cousin. And since Augustine's doctrine of the just war had become a familiar part of Christian morality,

Muhammad was probably aware of it. So it is hardly surprising that, as a man of the highest moral integrity, he abided by even stricter rules in the conduct of war. Thomas Aquinas and other medieval Christian scholars were almost undoubtedly familiar with the Muslim teaching on war; so it is hardly surprising that their criteria for a just war are to a great extent an exposition of the *sharia*. Thus we may regard Islam and Christianity as carriers of a common tradition concerning warfare.

In addition to their natural revulsion at the acts of Islamic terrorists, most devout Muslims feel disgusted at their hypocrisy. The terrorists claim to be loyal followers of the *sharia*, and at least two terrorist groups include the word *sharia* in their name. Yet even the simplest mind can see that terrorism is an affront to the *sharia*: it involves deceit, and it cannot help but kill and injure children, women and the elderly. So, although the precise mental state of terrorists is hard to fathom, it is hard to imagine that their motives for violence are as pure as Muhammad demanded; some twisted form of pride must surely drive them.

Yet combating modern terrorism presents novel and particular difficulties in applying the principles of just war. Terrorists are highly elusive, moving discreetly from place to place; and their financial backers are businessmen who are indistinguishable from other businessmen. Conventional military weaponry is designed to fight large armies whose identity is obvious. The occasional daring raid, based on good intelligence, may enable brave soldiers to hunt down and eliminate a few terrorists; but whole networks cannot be destroyed by this means. And raids based on incomplete intelligence are likely to slaughter the innocent. As for punitive attacks on those suspected of harboring terrorists, they not only kill the innocent along with the guilty; they also recruit more young men to the terrorist cause – as the British found in Afghanistan in the nineteenth century, and as President Clinton found after his raids on Afghanistan and Sudan in 1998. The whole of the West, and much of the rest of the world, was filled with righteous anger on September 11; but turning righteous anger into righteous warfare is agonizingly difficult.

There is comfort and strength, however, in the knowledge that in opposing terrorism the West has the *sharia* on its side. A few days after that fateful day, President Bush spoke of a 'crusade'. To many it seemed an unfortunate word, recalling the medieval wars between Christians and Muslims. But the president was justified in evoking religion. Christians and Muslims have a joint moral heritage that outlaws the killing and maiming of civilians in the conduct of war; and the killing and maiming of civilians, in order to spread fear, is the terrorist's sole aim.

The legacy

A S THE CENTURIES and millennia pass, civilizations and cultures rise and decline. Chinese and Indian civilizations glittered for well over a thousand years, but by the medieval period both were losing their brightness. Greek civilization shone with great intensity for a short period, and then was overtaken by the bolder and less subtle civilization centered on Rome. Two and a half centuries after the fall of Rome, Islamic civilization spread westwards across the Roman world, and then eastwards to India and beyond; and for almost a thousand years its achievements in all almost every sphere of human endeavor were dazzling. For the past two centuries the culture of western Europe and north America has been in the ascendant, and its achievements have been no less dazzling. And while a dominant people is generally reluctant to acknowledge its debts – indeed, is often unaware of them – each new civilization has borrowed much from earlier civilizations elsewhere.

Yet the nature of that interrelationship between peoples and cultures is changing rapidly. The West learned the scientific method from Islam, and it has used that method to develop, amongst many other things, technologies for communication that have shrunk the world. Radio and television, and more recently email and the internet, have made the peoples of the world familiar with one another. Thus knowledge and ideas, which in the past took decades and centuries to cross continents, now take months, days and minutes. And printing, a technology invented by the Chinese many centuries ago, has in western hands become vastly more versatile and economical, enabling scholars in every part of the world to share their insights and discoveries. Thus a kind of global civilization is developing that stands above individual nations and cultures, and exerts a growing influence on them.

This global civilization may be regarded as the joint legacy of Islam and the West. And since knowledge and ideas, intellectual insights and ideas, comprise the life-blood of any culture, every culture potentially stands to benefit.

Part 3:

'What can we do – politically?'
The politics of peace

The globalization of goods and capital

AT THE BEGINNING of the nineteenth century an English economist, David Ricardo, who had earned a small fortune as a banker, put forward a glorious vision of the world economy operating to every nation's advantage, making the entire population of the world richer. He offered clear and precise proofs for all his arguments, which seem incontrovertible. For about a century and a quarter his vision went virtually unquestioned, and guided policy-makers throughout the western world, even justifying the existence of the great empires amassed by Britain, France, Germany, Belgium and Holland. In the 1930s, in the midst of a global economic slump, another English economist, John Maynard Keynes, cast serious doubt on one half of Ricardo's vision. But by the 1960s a raft of American economists, led by Milton Friedman, were busily updating Ricardo's theories; and through the 1970s and early 80s they won growing support amongst policy-makers. Although few of their senior functionaries are aware of its intellectual pedigree, Ricardian economics infuses the two main international economic institutions, the World Trade Organization (WTO) and the International Monetary Fund (IMF). And Ricardo is the invisible guide in government finance and trade departments in America, Europe, and much of the rest of the planet.

The first half of Ricardo's vision is a theory of international trade, known as comparative advantage. For simplicity he imagined a world economy with two countries, Portugal and England, producing only two goods, cloth and wine. Portugal is better at producing both goods, in that it takes people fewer hours to produce a cask of wine and a bale of cloth in Portugal than it does in England. So one might imagine that the Portuguese would produce wine and cloth for themselves, and ignore England. But Ricardo pointed out that, if the difference in productivity is greater for one good than the other, it would be better for each country to specialize and trade. Thus if Portugal has a greater comparative advantage in wine than in cloth, both countries would gain by Portugal producing wine and England producing cloth – and for ships to carry cloth and wine between them.

The implications of this theory, which can be proved by quite a simple piece of mathematics, were, and still are, enormous. In the eighteenth century trade within Europe was subject to a complex network of tariffs, many of which were more than 25% of the value of the goods being traded. The purpose of the tariffs was to protect domestic industries from international competition, and to provide revenue for governments. Ricardo's theory showed, to the satisfaction of the British government, that these tariffs made Britain and her trading partners poorer, and reduced their rate of economic growth. So British officials from the 1820s onwards set out to negotiate the mutual abolition of tariffs with her trading partners; and if a particular country would not agree, Britain simply abolished its own tariffs on imports from that country. The astonishing success of the British economy soon convinced other European countries that Britain's policy was right; and they too became eager exponents of free trade.

Ricardo's theory also greatly accelerated the expansion of trade with India and the rest of Asia and the Middle East. Britain and the other European powers dismantled the various barriers to trade in the respective empires and spheres of influence. As a consequence the Asian and Middle Eastern economies became specialists in producing raw materials for European factories; and the factories exported a portion of their output back to Asia and the Middle East. When European explorers penetrated the African interior later in the nineteenth century, the European powers were soon scrambling to impose on its unsuspecting tribespeople the same Ricardian principles.

Above all, Ricardo presided over the astonishing expansion of the American economy, so that by the beginning of the twentieth century President Theodore Roosevelt could envisage the United States competing with, and soon overtaking, the old European nations as a world power. At first, like the Asian economies, north America specialized in producing primary products; but, having the same culture as Europe, it was easily able to emulate European industry. And the growth of American industry gave a further vital twist to the Ricardian scheme. The factories springing up, first on the eastern seaboard and then further west, required massive investment, which Americans at that time could not afford. So merchant banks and other financial intermediaries sprung up to channel surplus funds from Europe across the Atlantic. Thus to the globalization of trade was added the globalization of capital.

The second half of Ricardo's vision concerned the link between the supply and demand for goods. He espoused, and then in a novel way explained, a theory first enunciated by a French economist, Jean-Baptiste Say, that supply creates its own demand. This need not be true of a single firm, in that it may produce a good that no one wants; but according to Ricardo it is true of the economy as a whole. The main reason is that prices and wages adjust until total demand and supply are in equilibrium. Thus if total demand is too small to purchase all the goods being produced, prices and wages will fall until demand is sufficient. The main implication is that economies will always tend towards full employment: unemployed workers will be forced to lower their wages until they can produce goods cheap enough for people to buy.

Ricardo extended this theory of prices and wages to the international sphere. If an economy is importing more than it is exporting, money will flow out of it in order to pay for the excessive imports. With less money people will buy fewer goods, both imports and those produced at home. Firms in the home country will then be compelled to reduce prices, and workers reduce wages; and this in turn will make their goods more competitive internationally. Thus imports will fall, and exports rise, until the two are equal.

The inexorable growth of the European and American economies through the nineteenth and early twentieth centuries seemed to prove Ricardo's wisdom. No economies in history had enjoyed such expansion over so long a period; and levels of prosperity were being reached that far surpassed the wildest dreams of past generations. Admittedly there were occasional economic recessions, when for a short period output and employment would fall. But a boom soon followed, leading people to conclude that the capitalist economy was also inclined to oscillate. The underlying trend was always upwards.

This happy story was interrupted in the period following the First World War, when the capitalist economies entered a major slump from which they could not rise. Output plummeted and unemployment soared. Governments imposed tariffs in the hope of preserving their domestic industries; but since every tariff worsened the problem elsewhere, the net effect was to deepen the slump. Keynes, an economist whose genius equaled that of Ricardo, pronounced that the second half of Ricardo's vision was no longer correct; but he vigorously upheld and promoted the first half. He argued that workers through their trade unions were now able to resist reductions in wages; so firms, faced with falling demand, were unable to reduce prices, and instead had to reduce output. This in turn forced them to lay off workers, who then had less money to spend, causing demand, output and employment to fall even further. In Keynes's view the western economies were caught in this downward spiral; and they could only be lifted out of it by substantial government spending.

The New Deal of President Franklin Roosevelt was the first cautious application of Keynesian economics – although it began shortly before Keynes's main work was published. And in the three decades after the Second World War all western governments were committed to spending as much as was necessary to maintain full employment. Keynes himself remained a staunch supporter of free trade, condemning the imposition of trade tariffs as a 'beggar-my-neighbor' policy. And a global commitment to free trade was enshrined in the General Agreement on Tariffs and Trade, which later became the WTO.

By the 1970s the power of trade unions in the western world was starting to diminish. And through the 1980s labor markets changed radically: short and fixed term contracts become common; the typical size of plants and firms fell; and more and more people started their own businesses. As a result wages and incomes became flexible once more. Thus Keynes's critique lost its force, and Ricardian economics, with a few subtle tweaks, was restored to its full glory. Policy makers could again assure themselves that balanced government budgets and the elimination of trade barriers would be sufficient to enable everyone to become steadily richer. And the IMF, founded in 1944 by a group of economists led by Keynes to be a banker to governments, became – and remains – a tireless and dogmatic apostle of Ricardian economics to the countries of Asia, Africa and Latin America.

False assumptions

GANDHI, a student of history as well as a great religious teacher and shrewd political leader, observed that India in the eighteenth century was far more prosperous than Britain or the rest of Europe. It had a thriving rural economy that produced ample food, and the finest cotton and silk cloth in the world; and its surplus was so great that it financed the building of fabulous temples and mosques, and supported hosts of artists, writer and dancers. Small wonder that British adventurers came to India to make their fortunes. But, Gandhi said, free trade had ruined the Indian economy, so that by the end of the nineteenth century its cloth production had almost disappeared, it often could not feed itself, and its people spent much of their time in miserable idleness. Through the economic process analyzed by Ricardo, India had come to specialize in the growing of raw cotton and silk, while Britain specialized in spinning and weaving. But India's former spinners and weavers were unable to find alternative work; and since so much of India's land was now turned over to the supply of Britain's cotton mills, food was perennially scarce. Far from making India richer, free trade had simply made Britain richer at India own expense. The spinning wheel was for Gandhi the symbol of Indian independence; in his view independence was not merely a change of government, but withdrawal from the global system of trade, and a return to self-reliance.

While the details differ in each case, Gandhi's theory of

impoverishment through trade can be applied to most countries of Asia and Africa. A few Middle Eastern countries have been partially spared from poverty by the discovery of oil; but wealth from oil merely masks the underlying economic devastation, which will be exposed as soon as oil runs out or demand for it falls. Gandhi himself never grappled with Ricardo's logic; but if he had done so, he would quickly have seen that, while the logic itself is impeccable, its crucial underlying assumption is false. The theory of comparative advantage assumes that people can move quickly and easily from one occupation to another. In his hypothetical example spinners and weavers in Portugal learn the skills to make wine, while the workers in English vineyards learn how to use spinning-wheels and looms. In nineteenth century India, faced with cloth spun and woven in British factories, the rural spinners and weavers were, according to Ricardian theory, required to find work growing cotton and breeding silk worms. Unfortunately people frequently cannot acquire new skills, nor move to the places where these skills may need to be practiced; and when they fail to adapt and move, they become idle and impoverished. In India this situation was made even worse by the fact that the expansion of cotton growing and silk farming required little additional labor; instead, farms hitherto producing crops for local consumption simply shifted to cotton and silk.

At this point the second half of Ricardo's vision should apply: unemployed workers reduce their wages until they become cheap enough to employ. But if people are already living near the level of subsistence, there is little scope for wage reductions; and if there are few firms in existence with scope for expansion, even starvation wages will not help. Thus, instead of Ricardo's smooth return to full employment, there is Keynes's vicious downward spiral of falling demand and falling employment, causing demand and employment to fall even further. This was precisely what occurred to India through the nineteenth century, and continued into the twentieth. And it is the cruel dilemma that now faces much of the Middle East, large chunks of the rest of Asia, almost the whole of Africa, and most of Latin America.

So why can these poor countries not follow the American example of the nineteenth century, attracting capital from abroad? This is the prescription advocated by the IMF and the other current exponents of global capitalism. Indeed, they argue that in an age of transnational corporations and sophisticated financial money markets it should be relatively easy to lure foreign investors, eager to take advantage of low wages. And the experience of the so-called Asian tigers, such as South Korea, Malaysia and Thailand, seems to confirm this optimism. But when in the past fifteen years governments have taken every drop of the IMF medicine, the economic cure has still not occurred. The reason is quite simple and obvious. Modern manufacturing industry is now so mechanized, requiring a few skilled workers rather than armies of unskilled workers, that low wages make little difference to costs. It is far more important to be near the affluent markets of the West, so that designs can be altered rapidly in response to changing tastes and fashions, and the time taken to deliver the finished goods can be minimized. The small pockets of recent economic success in poor countries, such as Bangalore in south India, have depended on an existing pool of highly skilled workers able to speak fluent English; and these workers are engaged not on production lines in factories, but in research and software production.

Yet even when poor countries succeed in attracting western capital, experience shows it to be a mixed blessing. In the short run it provides jobs and incomes. But, whereas in America in the nineteenth century Americans themselves ran the new industries, today in Asia and Africa transnational corporations send their own managers and technicians to supervise their factories. Thus the transfer of skill and expertise is limited; and, worse still, the sense of inferiority to the West is deepened. Then, if local wages rise significantly or if changing global conditions induce changes in strategy, transnational corporations are free to dismantle their factories and move elsewhere, leaving the local people worse off than before.

It has been repeated so often in recent times that the rich in the world are getting richer and the poor are getting poorer, that we have almost come to regard this as an immutable economic law – equivalent to a natural law, such as night following day. Yet while the passing of night and day has a tranquil and unchanging rhythm, worsening inequality has a beat that grows louder and faster. As the plight of the poor becomes more desperate, so they become more willing to resort to desperate measures. Visitors to the West Bank and Gaza, witnessing the appalling conditions in which most Palestinians live, are no longer surprised at the flow of young men volunteering to be suicide bombers. And these Palestinian enclaves are positively luxurious compared with the destitution suffered by many hundreds of millions elsewhere across the Muslim world and beyond. If these destitute millions were unaware of western affluence, their resentment and anger, like that of Job in the Bible, might be directed against God. But most see pictures of the West on communal television sets; most hear on communal radio sets of western economic and political involvement in their countries; and many see western aid workers in expensive vehicles. So the West's relationship with them seems, in the stark image coined by Tolstoy, like a big fat man riding on the back of a small thin man, the big man occasionally reaching forward to put a morsel of food in the small man's mouth. And Islamic terrorism seems like the small man biting the tip of the big man's finger.

The globalization of people and expertise

UNTIL ABOUT two centuries ago trade between continents was minimal, confined to a few luxuries such as jewelry, fine silks, and spices; and even between neighboring countries trade involved only a negligible portion of total output. Yet the movement of people has always been huge. As far as scientists can tell, *homo sapiens* evolved in eastern Africa, and spread from there across the globe; and archeologists and historians tell us of many more recent migrations. For example, four millennia ago hundreds of thousands of Aryans moved from the central Asian steppes into India and Europe; and a later western movement from central Asia led ultimately to the fall of Rome. A millennium and a half ago Angles and Saxons spread from their German heartlands across the North Sea to Britain; then Vikings moved southwards from Scandinavia into Ireland, Britain and France. At the same time large groups from Iran and Syria were sailing to the Malabar coast of India. And since the sixteenth century emigrants from Europe have settled in vast numbers over three entire continents, Australasia, North and South America, largely displacing the existing inhabitants. These movements of population have often provoked violence; readers of the Bible are familiar with the battles between the immigrant Hebrews and the native Canaanites. But through a varying mixture of slaughter, inter-marriage, and territorial division peace has in most cases been established.

As people have migrated, so they have carried their skills and expertise across the world, and also learned skills from the people amongst whom they settle. Thus by about two millennia ago people throughout the Eurasian landmass had acquired the knowledge to forge metal tools, and to fire and glaze clay pots. The art of cooking, which makes food more digestible and thus led to great improvements in human health and strength, seems to have spread from China. And the most important skill of all, breeding large grains from small grass seeds, seems to have developed in the fertile crescent between the rivers Tigris and Euphrates. This marked the birth of agriculture, enabling food to be produced far more plentifully; and agricultural skills were taken across the world with remarkable speed, so the human population multiplied. The final victory of settled farming over nomadic herding occurred in the American wild west – a victory both celebrated and lamented in numerous Hollywood movies depicting the conflicts between homesteaders and ranchers.

Yet in the recent past, through a mixture of political action and entrepreneurial energy, the nature of globalization has been turned on its head. Whereas goods and capital were once virtually static, now they hurtle across the planet; and whereas people and skills once moved across the planet, now they are forced to be static. Western governments have taken pride in lifting all controls on the trade and investment; but they have imposed ever harsher measures against immigration. And just as the globalization of goods and capital has impoverished many countries in Asia and Africa, so the suppression of global movements of people has locked the populations of those countries in their poverty. This reverse globalization is assumed, and implicitly advocated, by Ricardo's theory of comparative advantage. In his hypothetical example the English would gain most by migrating to Portugal, where they could become more efficient in both cloth and wine production; but Ricardo disallows international migration, so people are compelled to endure the low efficiency of their homeland.

The specter of uncontrolled immigration from Africa and Asia strikes fear in the hearts of many westerners. While no one imagines that the battles between Hebrews and Canaanites will be re-enacted on the streets of Chicago, Birmingham and Munich, people envisage modern forms of civil tension and strife. They are anxious about their culture being radically altered by close proximity to people with an alien culture; they anticipate that wages will fall sharply as the supply of labor rises, so their own incomes will fall; they worry about a rise in crime; and they assume that the pressure on the various services financed by the government will be so large that their own access to these services will be hindered. Terrorism now adds an additional fear: that putative suicide bombers will slip in with the honest migrants. None of these fears is groundless. If there were a huge and sudden flood of tens of millions of immigrants, most of these fears would, to some degree and for a short period, be realized; and if there were no adequate checks, the terrorist's plans would in one respect be a little easier to accomplish. But there is no reason to expect a flood; and to protect itself from this possibility, immigration controls could be relaxed gradually. As for the putative terrorist, a warm welcome for his compatriots would make them less willing to shelter him, and more willing to provide the authorities with information.

In fact, western experience of immigration in modern times has been almost entirely positive. For example, Asian, African and West Indian immigration into Britain between 1950s and 70s has enlivened British culture. Hispanic immigrants into America, many of them illegal, have filled menial jobs that existing Americans have shunned; and illegal Slavic and Middle Eastern immigrants perform a similar economic function throughout western Europe. Once settled, immigrants often prove to be enterprising businessmen, creating jobs rather than lowering wages, and adding to the tax revenues from which public services are provided.

Immigrants are renowned for sending money home to their relatives. So immigrants from Asia and Africa would help to relieve the immediate poverty of their home countries. More importantly, many immigrants are keen eventually to return to their home countries in order to start businesses there, using their western earnings as capital, and putting the skills and expertise acquired in the West to more profitable use. Paradoxically, by making immigration legal, western countries would make it more likely that immigrants would return home, since they would know that, at any time they wished, they could come back to the West.

The ability of Asians and Africans to start businesses at home depends to a great extent on curbing the globalization of goods and capital. Three and a half centuries ago a wise political economist called William Petty advocated the use of tariffs to protect 'infant industries' from foreign competition; without them new enterprises might be drowned by cheap imports before they could become established. In the post-war period, with western approval, Japan erected a tariff wall behind which its devastated economy could recover; and a little later the Asian tigers all erected similar walls to encourage domestic industry. But a tariff wall need not be temporary, to be pulled down as soon as local firms can compete in world markets. Ricardian economics rightly predicts that, as soon as tariffs disappear, firms without comparative advantage will be destroyed. Rather a country, or group of neighboring countries, could have a permanent tariff wall, behind which they allow a multiplicity of different industries to develop, meeting the great bulk of local needs. Indeed, to see the success of such a policy, one need look no further than the European Union, which in essence is a customs union, with no internal barriers to trade, and a common external barrier; since its inception in 1957 the member countries have become largely self-reliant, and now enjoy a remarkable degree of both prosperity and stability. The EU is, of course, guilty of monstrous hypocrisy, since it strongly supports the WTO in its efforts to break down trade barriers elsewhere in the world. Countries in Asia and Africa would be wise to defy the WTO, and follow the EU's example.

In one respect, however, Europe remains vulnerable: while its goods markets are protected, its capital markets are open. Thus people living elsewhere in the world are free to own shares in European companies, open factories on European soil, and make speculative purchases of the euro currency; and they are free to sell their shares, close down their factories, and offload their euros. Happily for the people of Europe their economy is sufficiently solid and stable that when, for example, a Japanese transnational company closes down an electronics factory, the redundant workers can usually – but by no means always – find alternative jobs; and speculative sales of the euro, causing it to lose over 20% of its value in the two years after its launch, has caused little more than hurt pride. But the Asian tigers enjoy no such protection. When in 1997 there was a sudden loss of confidence amongst currency speculators, one currency after another collapsed; and since many companies were dependent on foreign loans valued in dollars, one company after another found itself insolvent. Countless families were cast into poverty, where many still remain. Admittedly this crisis exposed genuine weaknesses, particularly in the way in which local banks extended credit, which needed to be remedied. But it also exposed, for all to see, the folly of building an economic edifice on the shifting sands of global capital.

Three decades ago a distinguished economist, James Tobin, proposed that a modest tax be levied on foreign exchange transactions, in order to discourage currency speculation. Since that time, whenever the Tobin tax is mentioned in the media, the men who grow rich on currency speculation (there are very few women in this field) shake their heads, pronouncing it impractical because the currency markets are too complex for governments to monitor. Yet a few days after the attacks on New York and Washington it appeared that Islamic terrorists may have made vast sums by speculating on 'futures' in gold, airline shares and oil contracts. This can probably never be proved, because at present secrecy is too easy to maintain; and even if it is untrue, there is little doubt that terrorist funds slosh around the international financial system. So western governments, as part of their war on terrorism, have declared their determination to maintain permanent computerized checks on all financial transactions throughout the world. If governments can find ways of detecting the dirty dealings of Osama bin Laden and his cronies, they should have little problem in levying the Tobin tax.

Far more important that the Tobin tax, however, are controls on the ownership of shares and land, and on the raising of loans. Countries or groups of countries should require all businesses operating within their territory to be locally controlled; so there should be an upper limit on the proportion of shares held by people residing outside, and on the proportion of loan capital raised from outside. And people residing abroad should not be permitted to own land. Thus poor countries can build their economies on solid financial foundations.

Politics after September 11

THE MOST vibrant city in the world, the city that never sleeps, became not only somber and achingly sad in the aftermath of September 11, but also astonishingly gentle and generous. Car horns fell silent, truck and cab drivers no longer shouted abuse, young people escorted older people across the highway, and criminals restrained their larcenous instincts. Those who had lived in London through the blitz of 1940, and survived, were not surprised; when the people of a city or town suffer a collective tragedy, they draw together in mutual concern and support. And wartime London and New York share another, more subtle, moral attitude: stoic defiance, which excludes any desire for revenge. Londoners refused to be cowed, and yet had little hatred of the Germans raining down bombs; New Yorkers also remain unbowed, and also are surprisingly free of loathing for their cruel enemies. When Winston Churchill strode over the rubble in his boiler suit, he expressed this spirit in words of eloquent simplicity: 'London can take it.' Mayor Giuliani has expressed it in his calm resilience and honest dignity.

But, though the mood of London and New York are the same, the wider political context is wholly different. Londoners, and their fellow Brits, had a clear enemy, the Nazi regime led by Hitler, and they knew that Nazism had to be defeated by creating a more powerful army, navy and airforce than Hitler possessed. They also knew that once Nazism was defeated, they needed to make friends with Germany, and together build a peaceful Europe. New Yorkers, and their fellow Americans, have no clear enemy, since Islamic terrorism is hidden and elusive. Indeed, New York financiers are grimly aware that terrorists may be working in their midst; only insiders could have successfully traded in those gold, oil and share futures. And they know that a war against terrorism can have no victorious conclusion, after which the hand of friendship can be extended; when one part of the terrorist network has been defeated, other parts will remain a threat.

This dilemma, which is simultaneously moral and practical, confronts the whole of the western world, and even the whole of humanity. And it is equally difficult for those wanting to wage war and those wanting to make peace. If there can be no military victory, there can also be no treaty or settlement that ends hostility. In conventional negotiations between rival powers, each side presents demands, and then each side offers concessions, until finally an agreement is reached that is acceptable to both. But the Islamic terrorists are making no specific demands, and are willing to offer no concessions, because for them the enemy is western civilization itself, with its baleful domination of Muslim civilization. So while force of arms cannot defeat them, even the most generous diplomacy cannot appease them. The old political division between hawks and doves, warmongers and peacemakers, no longer applies.

Many people already understand this; and even though political rhetoric and action continues mainly to follow the old tune and rhythm, a different melody is already audible in the background. It has suddenly become possible to question the virtue of global capitalism without being regarded as a dangerous subversive or laughable crank. It is gradually becoming possible to suggest a more open and welcoming attitude to migration, without being dismissed as a utopian dreamer. Conventional assumptions are crumbling, and the political and economic values built upon them are showing cracks. As people speculate about terrorists acquiring nuclear devices and biological and chemical weapons, they know that a new way of ordering the world is urgently needed.

Other global issues are also being looked at afresh, most notably environmental pollution, which is ultimately an even greater threat to humanity than terrorism. Western governments have always been half-hearted about global warming, because they fear that any serious attempt to combat it could throw sand in the engine of global capitalism. But, since terrorism has now thrown whole rocks into that engine, this timidity now seems petty and absurd. The political impetus required to limit the globalization of goods and capital, and to allow the globalization of people and expertise, is the same kind of impetus required to regulate the emissions of greenhouse gases; and there is no shortage of practical ideas as to how this may be done, from direct controls to tradable permits. Moreover, once the people of individual countries become economically self-reliant, they will have a direct interest in conserving their resources.

Before September 11 the western economies led by America were already moving towards recession. Since September 11 people have lost much of their appetite for luxuries and frivolities; and as their consumption falls, so the recession may easily become a slump. It is not idle to imagine that western countries may follow the example of Japan where for the past decade people have been content with the material standard they have already attained, and simply save any additional income; and the likelihood of this would be greatly enhanced by any further terrorist attacks, even comparatively minor ones. The Japanese government has responded in the Keynesian manner, boosting government expenditure while keeping taxes down, and slashing interest rates; they have even reduced interest rates to nothing, and given away vouchers that can be exchanged at ordinary shops. And the early signs are that western governments and central banks intend to move in the same direction. But Japanese households have remained impassive; when they received the vouchers, they merely cut their expenditure of their own money by the equivalent amount. It seems possible, even likely, that westerners will be similarly reluctant to consume their way back to an economic boom. Besides, America and Britain both have such huge trade deficits that Keynesian policies, by increasing those deficits, would founder on the rocks of a currency collapse and subsequent inflation.

While Keynes was correct to condemn individual countries for imposing unilateral tariffs in the 1930s, international agreements on trade controls would boost economic activity. And if they were combined with anti-pollution controls, capital controls, and free migration, the economies of the world could enjoy a new kind of boom that steadily reduced inequality, and thus could be sustained. To begin to imagine such a boom, one may consider a single, vital industry, the production of automobiles. Suppose the governments of the world agreed that, over the coming twenty-five years, the use of fossil fuels in automobiles would be phased out; at the same time tariffs on the international trade of automobiles would be gradually raised, and capital controls would be imposed. Immediately automobile companies would recruit armies of researchers to develop new kinds of engines; and they would then build new factories to produce these engines. In the meantime to maximize their profits from the research, they would sell it to other countries at whatever price each country could pay; and new automobile factories would spring up across the world. If these engines were more expensive to run, public transport would become more competitive, and so would expand. And the countries of the Middle East currently dependent on oil – whose rulers have frittered most of the oil revenues away on lavish social provision for their people and obscene luxury for themselves – would have a compelling incentive to invest their remaining revenues in creating new industries to provide goods and jobs in the future.

If such a scenario seems a little fanciful, then one may take a dose of new realism from the latest *World Economic Outlook* by the IMF, published in late September, though written prior September 11. It concludes there is no 'significant relationship ... between capital liberalization and growth', adding that 'it would be a mistake for [poor] countries to think that involvement with global capital markets offer a magic, near-term fix for their problems.' When the IMF is having severe doubts about Ricardian economics – even before the catastrophe of September 11 – then the rest of us can safely assume that the Ricardian era is quickly passing.

After the end of the Cold War the American political scholar Samuel P Huntington argued that the most important disputes of the future would be between rival civilizations with antagonistic ideologies. As many commentators have commented, the attack of September 11 may presage the fulfillment of Huntington's prediction – the first major blow against western civilization by people with a quite different view of how human society should be organized. Despite the relative novelty of international terrorism as a means of warfare, history lends credence to this thesis. Civilizations – of which the West and Islamdom are classic examples – clash for one of two reasons: either one civilization wants the territory of the other; or one civilization feels the other civilization is exercising an unwelcome influence on its way of life. The spread of the Arab and Ottoman empires led to the first kind of clash, as did the Crusades; the rise of western imperialism had elements of both kinds of clash; modern Islamic militancy is a pure example of the second kind. The first kind of clash is resolved by one side vanquishing the other, or by a peace treaty. The second kind of clash is resolved by altering the nature of the relationship between the two civilizations.

Altering the relationship between the West and the rest of the world, including the Muslim countries, is the great political challenge of our time.

Towards political freedom

I N T H E mid eighteenth century the French philosopher, Jean-Jacques
Rousseau, famously began his treatise, *The Social Contract*, with
the words: 'Man was born free, and he is everywhere in chains.' He
then grappled with the relationship between individual and collective
freedom within society. He recognized that individuals have certain
economic freedoms, such as what goods to buy, what work to do, and
how to invest their wealth; but these freedoms are exercised within a
framework of laws that constrain and limit them. France in
Rousseau's time was ruled by a monarchy with the power to impose
laws, which Rousseau loathed; and he wondered how the making of
laws could itself become free. His answer lay in the concept of the
general will, in which individuals freely align their own wills with
that of the community as a whole, expressed through voting. He
proposed that the people should initially elect a parliament whose
members draft laws; these laws should then be accepted or rejected
by the people in a direct ballot. When a particular law is proposed,
some are likely to be in favor of it, and some against it; and vigorous
debate should occur. But as soon as a vote is taken, everyone should
willingly submit to the will of the majority.

Amongst the nations of the West only Switzerland follows
Rousseau's idea of the people voting on laws – although some states
in America, such as California, have frequent ballots on legal
amendments. In every other country the elected representatives both
draft and pass laws. And all western nations allow people to continue

expressing disapproval of laws even after they have come into force. Yet the principle of the general will, in which laws enacted by democratic means are binding on everyone, has been adopted throughout the West, and is the foundation of every western political constitution.

Islam, as we have seen, began to grapple with the relationship between individual and collective freedom twelve centuries earlier. Muhammad himself expressed the principle of the general will in his much-quoted saying: 'My community will never agree on an error.' At that time no system of popular voting had ever existed in any large country or empire; the system of democracy in ancient Athens, in which every male citizen attended the political gatherings, could only work in a single small city or town. Besides, even if the Muslim legal scholars had considered popular voting, they would quickly have dismissed it as impractical: the Arab empire was too large, communication was too slow and unreliable, and too many people were nomadic. So they put their trust in judges, who were required to be sensitive to popular opinion. Yet there is nothing in the *sharia* itself requiring that judges be the medium of the general will; and in the present age, when communication is quick and reliable, and almost everyone is settled, popular voting is surely a preferable medium. Indeed it is hard to imagine that the great al-Shafii would not have been delighted with modern forms of democracy.

It is tempting to say that the system of government is a matter for each country to determine for itself; so the fact that many Middle Eastern countries are highly autocratic, with rulers who habitually ignore popular opinion, should not concern anyone outside those countries themselves. This isolationist argument would perhaps be valid if populations were entirely static. But today most western nations have substantial numbers of Muslims, most of whose families originate from the Middle East; and it is important that they should feel that the system of government under which they live, and to which they must submit, is compatible with their religion. And if we are to negotiate greater freedom of movement between nations, then it becomes vital that some common political principles, which all reasonable people can accept, are agreed.

The atrocity of September 11 has been widely, and rightly, interpreted as an attack on democracy. In a democracy dissent is expressed in open debate and through voting; so any kind of intimidation, by which tiny majorities try to assert themselves over the general will, is a dagger aimed at democracy's heart. It follows that the war against terrorism is in defense of democracy. Yet the conduct of this war involves a profound moral and political contradiction. It can only be seriously waged with the cooperation of highly undemocratic governments in the Middle East; and in the face of autocracy terrorism is, in many people's eyes, a valid form of resistance. Indeed the West has a long, and often honorable, tradition of supporting terrorism in the name of freedom. Many westerners supported the terrorist campaign conducted by the African National Congress against the apartheid regime of South Africa; and, when the ANC's leader, Nelson Mandela, who had been imprisoned for terrorist activities, was elected president of South Africa, the whole world applauded. Going further back, the fighters in the French Resistance fought the Nazi occupation of their country by means of terrorism, which was the only strategy at their disposal; and they are lauded as heroes. And in the 1980s the American and British governments gave financial and military support to the *mujahideen* (holy warriors), who included Osama bin Laden, in their guerilla war against the Soviet-backed regime in Kabul; British commandoes even instructed them in terrorism's dark arts.

In the heat of crisis one enemy's enemies quickly becomes one's friend; so several autocratic Middle Eastern regimes, which are themselves threatened by Islamic militants, have been welcomed as supporters in the war against terrorism. But as American leaders never tire of repeating, this war will not be over in five days, five months, or even five years; it is a long, long war. And a vital element in ultimate victory is that all the peoples of the Middle East and beyond must enjoy political freedom; only then does terrorism lose its moral and persuasive force. As the multiplicity of constitutional arrangements in the West demonstrates, there is no single form that freedom must take; and in every country of the world the cultural traditions and the ethnic mix are different, with differing political implications. But by one means or another the principle of the general will, enunciated by Muhammad and Rousseau, must be enacted.

Thus the war against terrorism is not ultimately a matter of military incursions and protective action; it is matter of diplomacy and negotiation, argument and discussion. Of course, autocratic regimes will resist change. But, even if they care nothing for freedom, all autocrats want their countries to prosper, if only to allay popular discontent; and they look with dismay and fear at the poverty in which most of their people live. This gives power to the forces of freedom. By proposing to turn globalization on its head, replacing the globalization of goods and capital with the globalization of people and knowledge, the West would offer a route to prosperity – and to dignity. And this new form of globalization depends on the spread of freedom.

On the path to freedom the conflict between the Israelis and Palestinians is the largest boulder. How, the leaders and the people alike of the Middle East ask, can the West be sincere in its espousal of freedom when it supports the Israeli oppression of the Palestinian Arabs? Even the most generous proposals ever offered by the Israelis go only a short way to satisfying Palestinian demands. But if this conflict is utterly intractable in the present political order, it begins to become soluble in the new political order of universal freedom. And the founding father of Zionism, Theodor Herzl, would heartily approve the new order. He wanted a united Palestine, in which Jew and Muslim are equal and free under the law; and he understood that such a political order conformed to the best traditions of Judaism and Islam alike. Modern Israelis would understandably view with skepticism any return to the original Zionist vision; all the Arab states around them are autocratic, so they would distrust the commitment of Palestinian Arabs to democracy. But if the whole of the Middle East were moving towards democracy, the picture would be transformed. Thus a permanent resolution of the Israeli-Palestinian conflict is both a crucial means of achieving the new political order, and a priceless prize of its achievement.

Part 4:

'What can we do –
religiously?'
The religion of peace

The globalization of creeds and sects

WHEN PAUL of Tarsus set out across the eastern Mediterranean, he had a story to tell, a piece of good news. It was that a man had died on a cross, and then had risen back to life. He drew several conclusions from this story, the main one of which is that it offers an image of human fulfillment: 'We are buried with Christ, so that as he was raised from the dead by the glory of the Father, we too might walk in newness of life.' And he devoted much of his writings to describing 'newness of life'. Those risen with Christ, according to Paul, never lie or cheat, they always give generously to those in need, they restrain their anger and suppress their pride, they welcome strangers into their homes, they are faithful in marriage and they are gentle with their children. None of these moral demands would have appeared unusual or novel to his readers; indeed, as he himself wrote, he was merely outlining the moral laws 'written on all people's hearts.' And he regarded moral evil as an inner bond, an addiction, from which people must be liberated. When later theologians have scoured his writings for a creed, they have found only a single, simple sentence that appears twice in slightly different forms: Jesus Christ is Lord.

A few decades after Paul's hectic travels a man called John grappled with the nature of this man who had died and risen again. He was steeped in the philosophy of the Greek Stoics, which had passed into Jewish thought through Philo, a member of the large Jewish community in Alexandria. John took from Philo the concept of *Logos*, usually translated as Word, which signifies divine energy present throughout the world and the universe, and which creates and sustains every object and living being. A similar concept, referred to as 'wisdom', appears in the later writings of the Jewish Bible (the Old Testament, as Christians call it): Wisdom, according to the Book of Proverbs, was God's agent in the process of creation, and continues to dwell in human minds. According to John, Jesus Christ was *Logos* made flesh: he was in perfect union with the Word, and thence completely free from the bonds of evil.

Judging from his sayings contained in the four Gospels, Jesus sometimes saw himself as a reformer trying to purify the religion of his fellow Jews, and sometimes as the conveyor of a message to the wider world. In the immediate aftermath of his death his followers regarded themselves as a reforming sect within Judaism, and stuck closely to the Jewish laws on such matters as food and circumcision. Paul himself only became a follower some time after Christ's death, and appears largely ignorant of Christ's teaching, referring directly to it only once. But he was convinced that the manner of Christ's death and resurrection had global significance; and during a stormy meeting in Jerusalem he persuaded the sect's leaders to support him in his mission. Thus Christianity, as interpreted by Paul, became the first religion with explicit global ambitions.

Paul established small communities of Christians in major cities; and while he personally remained in touch with them through letters, they functioned independently. Indeed, he acknowledged that he had no authority to issue orders to them, and could only guide them by persuasion. Through the second and third centuries the leaders of communities gradually acquired more power; and the leaders of communities in particular regions gathered occasionally to form a common view on controversial issues. Also the leadership approved particular writings, which became known as the New

Testament, as authoritative. In the fourth century, however, this network of groups was welded together into a huge organization; the leaders of this organization – the bishops – began to distill the Christian message into a series of verbal formulae. The impetus for this process was the decision by the emperor Constantine to make Christianity the official religion of the Roman empire, seeing it as an antidote to the political and social forces that were pulling the empire apart. And he offered the bishops a generous deal that they were delighted to accept: that the state would give material support to the Christian church, and allow it complete freedom to accumulate wealth; in return the church should uphold the authority of the state, declaring it to be divinely sanctioned.

Constantine himself was instrumental in convening the first council of bishops from throughout Christendom, held in Nicea in Asia Minor in the year 325; and the bishops proved so quarrelsome that he agreed to preside over some of their debates. The council finally agreed that Jesus Christ was not merely a human, but was also divine. And at subsequent councils the bishops hammered out a set of formulae, known as the Nicene Creed, that in their view defined the Christian faith. This in large part relates the story of Christ as a divine man. But crucially it declares that the church is uniquely guided by Christ's Spirit, and thus has absolute authority on doctrinal matters. Thus the relationship between organization and belief was made circular: the church tells Christians what to believe; and to be Christian a person must belong to the church.

Islam was the second religion with global ambitions. The Quran itself has the same ambivalence towards the wider world as the Gospels. To a great degree Muhammad is presented as a reformer, purifying Arabian religion of idolatry and other corrupt practices, and restoring its ancient faith. But the Quran also makes clear that all religions, when they are purified, are essentially the same; so its message is universal. This ambivalence extends to Muhammad's relationship with God. Mainly he is presented as one of many prophets; in each place and in every age God calls particular individuals to proclaim his message, and Muhammad is the individual chosen by God at that moment to proclaim his message in Arabia. But there are also suggestions that he is the final prophet, with a message for all places at all times.

Following the death of Muhammad, Islam made the transition from local sect to vast organization, which took Christianity three centuries, in only a few years. During his lifetime military necessity had forced Muhammad to create the concept of the Islamic community, the *umma*, comprising all those joined his campaign to defeat his persecutors in Mecca; and the importance of the *umma* is stressed within the Quran. In the process Muhammad extended the notion of *jihad* from a purely spiritual struggle to liberate oneself from evil, to a political struggle to liberate society from the control of evil people. After his death the *umma* became the vehicle both for spreading the spiritual message of Islam, and for extending its political power. And in place of the charismatic authority of Muhammad a hierarchy was instituted, with the caliph at its head, whose task was to uphold Islamic religion, and to maintain political control over Muslims and their territory. Thus the relationship between organization and belief was again made circular: a Muslim is someone who belongs to the *umma* and accepts its authority; and the *umma* consists of all who believe in Islam.

False assumptions

AT THE START of the fifth century the famous theologian and bishop, Augustine of Hippo, authorized the first specifically religious war that history records. The enemy was a group of Christians in north Africa known as Donatists, after their founder Donatus. They believed that the church hierarchy was entirely unnecessary, because individuals can receive direct guidance from God. They also said that religious hierarchies are endemically prone to corruption, because people given spiritual power are liable to become proud and arrogant, and because they can easily manipulate those beneath them to give them money. Augustine saw clearly that such views posed a threat to the very existence of the church as an organization, and thence to the entire corpus of doctrines that the church promulgates. He could not deny that many bishops were indeed corrupt, since this was only too obvious; but he argued that the sins of individual bishops did not undermine their corporate authority. And since the state was now the protector of the church, Augustine said that it had a duty to suppress the Donatists by force. So in 405 Donatism was outlawed, and soldiers began rounding up its defenseless adherents. Happily the political leaders had the wisdom not to kill any Donatists, for fear of creating martyrs; instead they confiscated all property owned by them, and imposed heavy fines. But a grim precedent had been set.

For the next thirteen centuries religious wars, some marked by the most appalling brutality and carnage, raged within Christendom.

Their purpose, like the original war against Donatism, was invariably to stamp out heresy. And the common feature of all heresies was that, implicitly or explicitly, they threatened the authority of the church in defining Christian belief; indeed, the word 'heresy' derives from a Greek word meaning 'freedom of choice'. Some heresies, like that promoted by Arius, denied the divinity of Jesus Christ; and if Jesus is merely human, then his Spirit cannot guarantee the truth of the church's teaching. Some, like that promoted by Abelard, denied the uniqueness of Christ, and so undermined the church's claim to have a monopoly of the truth. Some, like that of Pelagius, asserted that salvation is purely a matter of making good moral choices, so there is no need for theological doctrines. And many, like that of Donatus, asserted the ability of all Christians to communicate directly with God, making the church hierarchy redundant.

The most bitter of the wars against heresy was the last; and it had an extra twist in that, to some degree, it was between two rival views of ecclesiastical authority. The forerunners of the Protestants, such as John Huss in the early fifteenth century, held views similar to those of the Donatists. But the great Protestant leaders of the following century, in particular Martin Luther and John Calvin, looked back to Augustine as their theological inspiration. They asserted that the church had deviated from its original teaching, as contained in the Gospels and letters of Paul, and as interpreted by its early theologians, Augustine pre-eminent among them. In essence they proposed simplifying the hierarchy, and cleansing the church's teaching of the doctrines it had accumulated since Augustine's time. To the pope in Rome the complex hierarchy of which he stood at the apex, with its several tiers and its cumbersome procedures, was divinely sanctioned; and to question any of its doctrinal pronouncements was to cast doubt on its authority, and hence on all doctrines. So Europe divided, and then took up arms.

Islam has its own similar record of internal dissent and conflict. By the early eighth century, less than a hundred years after Muhammad's death, an eminent scholar Hasan al-Basr was criticizing the greed and hypocrisy of the senior clergy, who took pleasure in telling the people how to behave and what to believe, but who themselves were utterly unscrupulous and materialistic. A few decades later the Sufi movement began. The first known Sufi was a woman called Rabia, who went to live in the desert, and devoted herself to attaining mystical union with God. People soon flocked to see her, sensing a spiritual warmth within her that was absent from the clergy; and she openly criticized the clergy for using the fear of hell as a means of enforcing their authority. By the time Rabia died in 801 there were hundreds of Sufi mystics, some living in solitude, and some traveling from place to place teaching all who would listen. Their message was similar to that of the Donatists, that every individual can receive direct guidance and comfort from God. Therefore the clergy, who interpret and expound the Quran, are actually barriers to true religion; instead we need spiritual guides who can show us how to open our souls to the divine spirit. The most famous of the early Sufis was Hallaj, who taught that God dwells within every person – so every person is divine. To emphasize his conviction he frequently declared: 'I am the Truth.' This eventually so enraged the caliphs and senior clergy in Baghdad that they arrested and crucified him.

Despite frequent efforts to suppress it, the Sufi movement has continued to this day; and it was mainly Sufis that carried Islam – their mystical version of it – to west Africa, India and south-east Asia. However, the deepest division within Islam is between Sunni and Shii; and, as with Protestantism and Catholicism within Christianity, each accuses the other of heresy. The original split occurred late in the eighth century over the way in which the Muslim community should be ruled: the Sunni, who have always formed the majority, assert that the *sharia* is the ultimate source of authority, while the Shii place their trust in divinely-inspired human leaders. Beyond this lies a further division on their view of history: the Sunni believe that the ultimate destiny of Islam is to rule the world, whereas the Shii regard Muslims as a righteous minority awaiting the coming of a messianic figure – the *Mahdi* – who will usher in a society of perfect justice. Like Catholics and Protestants, Sunni and Shia have a long history of mutual persecution; recent examples are the ruthless slaughter by the Taliban and Saddam Hussein of the Shii minorities in their respective countries, and the oppression by the Iranian regime of its Sunni minority.

Over and above the conflicts within Christianity and Islam, there is, of course, the long history of bloodshed between them. As two rival religions, each with a mission to convert the world to its beliefs, their competition has occasionally been respectful and friendly. But these times have been the exception. More often mutual contempt has spurred them; and contempt has often turned to violence.

Yet this enmity within and between the two religions has been based on a false assumption: that there are ultimate truths capable of being defined and encapsulated in words. Organized Christianity, in both its Catholic and Protestant forms, and organized Islam, in both its Sunni and Shii forms, may properly be described as fundamentalist: they have fundamental doctrines that their members are required to accept; and they claim to base these on a holy book, the New Testament for Christians and the Quran for Muslims, whose text uniquely contains the fullness of truth. This primary false assumption is bound up with a secondary one: that a human organization has the authority to pronounce the truth. For Christians it is the organization that validated the holy book; for Muslims the organization's power is held to derive from the holy book. Donatism, Pelagianism and Arianism within Christianity, and the Sufism within Islam, are heresies because they oppose these assumptions.

For many orthodox Christians and Muslims religion itself is unimaginable without clear doctrines and authoritative organizations. Yet Hinduism comprises numerous organizations, with varying religious ideas, which co-exist in mutual respect; and the ancient Hindu religious books, such as the Upanishads, specifically deny that truth can be expressed in words. The great Taoist teachers, such as Lao Tzu and Chuang Tzu, express the view that religious organizations are dangerous and harmful. The Buddha used words as a means of carrying the human mind beyond words. Similar attitudes are found in many of the greatest Muslim and Christian philosophers, who show how priceless wisdom and insight can be gained from the Quran and the New Testament, without making the words themselves objects of veneration. For al-Razi such books are like signposts, showing the mind the way to the truth; for Avicenna their words are like windows, through which we see the truth beyond; and for Averroes holy books are simply one type of spiritual food amongst many, to be tasted when the soul is hungry for it. In the nineteenth century Christian theologians caught up with these Islamic intellectual athletes. Friederich Schleiermaher, for example, wrote: 'Religion is no kind of slavery, no kind of captivity; it is the place where you can be yourself – and the desire to be yourself is the beginning of faith.' He reinterpreted the entire body of religious doctrine in terms of psychological experience, showing how it can be a means of genuine personal fulfillment. A century later Dietrich Bonhoeffer, awaiting death in a Nazi prison, wrote of his contempt for 'religious people who bring God onto the scene as the apparent solution to insoluble problems'; and he advocated 'religionless Christianity' which 'simply means being a person – the person that God creates in us.'

The globalization of wisdom and symbols

IN PAST ERAS, when science had not yet discovered the complexity, enormity and antiquity of the universe, it was plausible to think that some overarching truths about existence could be expressed in verbal form. And when Islam and Christianity mostly occupied different parts of the globe, and when communication between them was intermittent and slow, it was relatively easy for their leaders to claim a monopoly of these truths. Yet in most western countries today members of different religious groups live side by side; and books and electronic media constantly remind us of the multiplicity of religious beliefs and practices. So it seems inherently unlikely that one religion is right, while all the others are wrong. Moreover, we are now aware that our species is one of hundreds of thousands, our planet is one of millions, and that the universe is billions of years old. So we are compelled to admit that our minds can only comprehend a tiny fraction of existence. Hence the doctrines of organized Christianity and Islam have quite simply been rendered absurd; indeed, acceptance of religious dogma of any kind involves intellectual dishonesty.

It is tempting, therefore, to dismiss religion as outdated. And, in the light of the bloodshed caused by religious doctrines, it is doubly tempting to oppose the very existence of religion. The outrage of September 11 is merely the latest vile crime against humanity conducted in the name of some human conception of God; surely it is time to destroy the sources of all conceptions of God. Yet human beings seem innately religious. Religious rituals and symbols of some kind have existed in every known human society; and spiritual teachers of some kind are everywhere accorded respect, and their wisdom sought. Certainly organized religion has declined steeply in Europe over the past century or more, and, although less marked, it has also declined in America; but interest in religion generally is more lively than ever. Stamping out religion is no more realistic than stamping out sex; and, just as we make a moral distinction between good sexual relationships and bad, so we must distinguish between good religion and bad. In other words, having dismissed the truth claims of religion, we must make pragmatic judgments about it in the same way that we make pragmatic judgments about political policies.

In order to make such judgments, we must first determine the essence of religion as a human phenomenon. In countries where Christianity, Islam or Judaism has been predominant, it may seem that the common feature of all religion is belief in one or more supernatural beings. Yet Buddhism, Taoism and some forms of Hinduism have no such belief; and Jainism is explicitly atheist. And the gods of many tribal African and Amerindian religions are so human in character that their activities are often best understood as parables. A better definition is that religion is concerned with people's inner being – their emotions and attitudes – and religious rituals and symbols exist to exert some kind of influence on how people feel and think. Thus while economic and political activity are directed towards changing our environment, religion is directed towards changing ourselves. Such a definition includes every religion; it also includes counseling and other forms of psychotherapy that have traditionally occurred within the orbit of religion, although they do not require any specific religious conviction or context.

With this broad definition it becomes quite simple to distinguish good and bad religion. Bad religion nurtures bigotry and contempt, while good religion nurtures tolerance and love. And this distinction is equally simple to apply. The religion motivating the terrorist hijackers on September 11 is manifestly bad; so also are the forms of Catholicism and Protestantism that fuel hatred in Ireland; so also are the forms of Judaism and Islam that fuel animosity between Israeli and Palestinian; and so also is any religion, in any mosque, church, synagogue or temple, that makes its adherents feel superior to others, because, as every great religious master has taught, spiritual pride and moral self satisfaction are the parents of bigotry and contempt. Some religious doctrines, and some religious organizations promulgating doctrines, can be relatively innocuous. But the history of Christianity and Islam shows that organized, doctrinal religion has an inherent tendency towards evil.

This tendency is rooted in the nature of both doctrines and organizations. By giving people the impression that they already possess truth, doctrines convey to them that they have no need to change; mere belief in the doctrines is sufficient. This is even made explicit in Protestantism, especially its Calvinist version, which holds that individuals are predestined to be either saved or damned; and holding the correct beliefs is a certain sign of salvation. Thus doctrines promote pride and self-satisfaction. Members of organizations, and especially leaders, tend to judge their success by their rate of expansion; and for religious organizations expansion implies acquiring more members. So every religious organization tends to see other religious organization as rivals that should be defeated and destroyed. And inevitably they often use their rituals and symbols to whip up bigotry and contempt towards any creed but their own.

Within every religious tradition we can also find countless

examples of goodness, not only within religious groups, but also reaching out beyond them. Jesus and Muhammad are themselves shining examples, both of whom showed kindness and generosity to anyone and everyone. And amongst those within Christianity and Islam who are revered as saints, the most popular are those like Francis of Assisi who had no interest in rising up the religious hierarchy, but were aflame with love for all humanity. Indeed, the sole justification for organized religion is that it helps to keep alive the memory of men and women whose goodness transcended all kinds of religious organization.

Despite the poor communication of past eras, religious insights managed to travel from one country to another, and from one continent to another. The interchange between Christianity and Islam from the very inception of Islam provides one example. Another example is the way in which Buddhism fused with the Confucian and Taoist traditions in China, renewing them both. And a little earlier Zoroastrian ideas spread from eastern Iran to stimulate Greek and Roman religious ideas, and to foster the spirit within Judaism that found its fullest expression in the teachings of Jesus and Paul. While the globalization of creeds and sects has a long history of enmity, the globalization of religious wisdom has an equally long history of mutual enrichment. And the far better communication of the present era, which helps to discredit sectarian globalization, hugely enhances the opportunities for spiritual globalization.

Happily these opportunities are being seized. People visit the buildings and enjoy the art of every religious tradition without discrimination. They read a spiritual article or book for the truths it might contain, regardless of the religious background of the author. The Buddha sitting in meditation has become as familiar an icon as Christ hanging from the cross. People are as happy to celebrate Arabic calligraphy as medieval stained glass. Far from being seen as an affront to the familiar church steeples, a minaret in a western city is welcomed as a sign of spiritual diversity. The more spiritual wells there are from which they can drink, so people surmise, the better their inner thirst will be quenched.

Religion after September 11

'WHAT WE SAW on Tuesday,' the Rev Jerry Falwell, a leading Christian evangelist, opined on television a few days later, 'could be miniscule if in fact God continues to lift the curtain and allow the enemies of America to give us probably what we deserve.' His friend Pat Robertson, another well-known evangelist, agreed. Jerry Falwell continued: 'I really believe that the pagans and the abortionists and the feminists and the gays and lesbians who are actively trying to make an alternative lifestyle ... all of them who have tried to secularize America, I point the finger in their face and say, "You helped this to happen."' Falwell and Robertson were expressing a religious attitude that in varying forms is familiar to Christian and Muslim worshippers everywhere: that God punishes those who do not believe in him and ignore his will. Indeed this view is implicit in the very notion of organized religion: the fear of some kind of divine retribution, and the hope of divine reward, is the ultimate reason why people adhere to religious doctrines for which there is no compelling evidence.

While few people would regard Falwell's remarks as tactful in the context – and he himself later issued a statement that seemingly contradicted them – it is possible that the kind of religion represented by him will experience a boom in response to the terrorist outrage. Certainly in the immediate aftermath congregations in churches swelled as people sought comfort and reassurance. But it is equally possible that, as people reflect, there may be a growing revulsion against organized religion. The suicidal hijackers exposed, if it needed exposing, the cruel logic of fundamentalist Islam; and Jerry Falwell showed that doctrinal Christianity follows a very similar cruel logic. No one doubts the logic itself, which, like that of Ricardian economics, is impeccable; but its underlying assumptions are both highly dubious, like Ricardo's, and also morally repugnant.

When people have replayed in their minds the television pictures of September 11, many have surely cried out to themselves: 'How can God allow this?' And some have equally surely asked the corollary: 'How can there be a God if things like this happen?' Thus they find themselves grappling with an issue that has nagged remorselessly at both Christianity and Islam every since they began to define their beliefs: the problem of evil. At the center of their respective creeds both Christianity and Islam, in common with Judaism, assert the existence of a supreme being – God, Allah, Yahweh – who is omniscient and omnipotent, encompassing all knowledge and power. Yet the existence of evil – and there has never been a more vivid image of evil than airplanes being deliberately flown into the World Trade Center – suggests that God is morally neutral, with no preference for good over evil. The only other explanations are that God cannot foresee evil, and hence is not omniscient, or cannot prevent it, and hence is not omnipotent; but these explanations amount to a denial of the very existence of God. Both Christian and Muslim theologians have tried to surmount this problem by suggesting that God deliberately limits his power and knowledge, in order to allow human beings some degree of freedom. But why, we are driven to ask, would God wish to limit his freedom if the consequences are so ghastly?

Thus people might quite reasonably turn away entirely from the Christian and Muslim conception of God. They might join with Nietzsche in declaring that God – the omniscient, omnipotent God of the monotheistic religions – is dead. And they might add that he deserves to die.

The apologists for organized Christianity and Islam have their reply, which has been repeated many times in the past: terrible evil and suffering has always existed, and yet their respective religions have survived; indeed, in times of particular suffering, such as the Black Death in the fourteenth century, their religions have thrived. But this complacency is misplaced. In the first place, heresies, which discard doctrines and organizational hierarchies, have generally proved more popular than orthodoxy; and in the fourteenth century heretical religion enjoyed a particular boom. Orthodoxy has only prevailed by allying itself with political power, which it has used to suppress heresies by force; but this option is now closed – the Taliban is perhaps the only regime in the world that continues to have a formal policy of massacring heretics. More importantly, the wider social and intellectual context has changed: local religious monopolies have been broken beyond repair by modern communications; and the very notion of religious doctrine has been discredited.

In the West the rejection of organized religion would have a psychological connection with the reduction of frivolous and indulgent consumption that may be the most visible economic consequence of September 11. Since organized religion by its nature tends to be bad, promoting bigotry and contempt, it leaves people restless and unfulfilled; and they try to assuage these unhappy feelings through the acquisition of goods and through expensive amusements. When good heretical religion takes its place, it brings over time inner peace and serenity; and hence people are content with fewer goods and simpler pleasures.

In the Muslim world the adoption of the right globalization policies to create prosperity would hasten the rejection of organized religion, and thence progressively weaken the grip of militant Islam. As people rise out of poverty and acquire a fuller education, and as they have better access to the modern means of communication, so the implausibility of organized religion will become more and more manifest, and the authority wielded by the religious authorities will lose its legitimacy.

Towards religious freedom

SCATTERED across the countryside of rural India there are innumerable temples and shrines. People visit these temples and shrines as and when they feel inclined; and they contribute money for their maintenance. Generally a few priests live nearby, who perform ceremonies of various kinds; and they go out from time to time to conduct weddings and funerals. The priests also farm some land or ply some craft, so they do not need to beg from worshippers. Some temples and shrines are entirely independent, and some belong to one of the many Hindu sects. But there is little rivalry between one temple and another, and between one sect and another; and many people enjoy visiting a variety of different types of temple.

In addition to the temples there are ashrams, where people go for spiritual teaching and advice. Ashrams come into being when a particular individual – a man or woman – gains a reputation for great wisdom. People are willing to travel a great distance to visit a teacher – a *guru* – whose style and insights appeal to them; and they build hostels near the teacher's house where they can stay. In many cases the ashram dies with the teacher; but sometimes one teacher appoints another as successor. A few teachers are mobile, wandering endlessly from place to place; so the spiritual pupils of such a teacher may spend a few days or weeks each year wandering alongside – or may decide to wander permanently in the teacher's shadow.

In the far southwest of India there are also small churches, belonging to a Christian group that probably dates back to the third century. This group has come to be regarded almost as another Hindu sect; and its members feel little inhibition about visiting Hindu temples, while many local Hindus are happy from time to time to worship in a church. There are a few Christian ashrams where Jesus Christ is presented as the *guru*. In some places Muslim mosques also fit harmoniously into this religious patchwork. Islam was originally brought to rural India by Sufis, who offered it simply as another spiritual path that people may choose to follow. In the cities of north India under the Mughal empire there was economic and political pressure on people to convert to Islam; but in the remoter regions people became Muslim if they happened to be drawn to Sufi teaching.

Sadly in certain parts of India in recent decades Hinduism has acquired a militant face. Indeed, it was a militant Hindu that assassinated Gandhi, hating him for the respect and love he showed towards all religions. To some degree Hinduism learnt the spirit of militancy from the Christian missionaries who, from the sixteenth century onwards, were bent on tearing people from their religious and cultural roots, and converting them to a quite different way of life. And to militant Christianity and Hinduism has now been added militant Islam. But many parts of the countryside have so far been spared these poisons; so they continue to offer an example of how free, open religion may work.

The antiquity of this example is attested in various texts, including the Buddhist scriptures. The Buddha was a wandering teacher in northern India with a substantial number of followers wandering with him. When he arrived at a town or village, he settled for a few days just outside, so that individuals living there were free to come and meet him. He never criticized the temples, and treated their priests with courtesy; he also happily entered into conversation and debate with other spiritual teachers. When people decided to acknowledge him as their *guru*, while remaining in their homes, he expected them also to remain loyal to their local temple. Justification for free, open religion is given in the *Bhagavad Gita*, an ancient Hindu text that commands almost universal respect: 'There is no distinction between one religion and another. People may worship in any form they wish; the form of worship does not matter. What matters is the quality of love that religion nurtures.'

If opinion polls are to be believed, this is the approach to religion that many, probably most, people in the West now favor. They have already broken the shackles of organized religion and verbal doctrines – or probably never wore those shackles, since their parents or grandparents threw them off. Yet they feel the need for religion, and want to satisfy that need without putting the shackles back on. The events of September 11 have both increased their dread of spiritual bonds, and increased their hunger for spiritual food. At present this hunger is being satisfied by new teaching centers, and by books and magazines; people are also feeding their souls by visits – pilgrimages – to churches and other sacred places. As yet, however, the conduct of worship, and the control of churches, remains almost entirely in the hands of doctrinal religious organizations. Our two greatest spiritual challenges are to find rituals and symbols that can uplift and transform people, while requiring no formal belief on their part; and to hand to popular control the places where rituals are traditionally enacted, and which are themselves powerful and benign symbols.

To a superficial observer the Muslim world appears still to be chained fast to doctrinal religion; and the publicity gained by militant Islam gives the impression that the chains are tightening. Yet in Muslim countries where free votes are taken, militant political parties obtain minimal support; and western journalists and academics working in Muslim countries consistently report that most people have very moderate religious views. There is widespread antagonism to western economic and political domination; and the appeal of Islamic militancy, such as it is, lies not in its religious convictions, but in offering a concrete means of expressing this antagonism. So as and when political and economic equality is achieved, the appeal will evaporate. And the Muslim world is better placed than the West to find free and open forms of religion, because Sufism has remained far more vigorous than any of the Christian heresies.

When religions are free, they happily trade their symbols; Hindu sects are so open to new symbols that many temples and Hindu homes have pictures of Jesus and the Virgin Mary, and hang star-shaped lanterns at Christmas. Thus we can look forward to growing artistic enrichment in western religion in the coming decades. But we may tentatively suggest a simple form that itself symbolizes free and open religion: the figure O. This, of course, stands for zero; and in free and open religion there are no beliefs. It also stands for the world; the fruit of free and open religion is a sense of loving unity with all humanity and all that lives.

Conclusion: freedom to live in peace

WE MAY assume that the primary aim of the terrorists on September 11 was to spread terror; and in this they succeeded beyond all measure. And as the outward signs of terror gradually fade with the passing weeks and months, it remains just below the surface, ready to erupt with even greater force as and when another terrorist attack is perpetrated.

This fear cannot honestly be assuaged by protective measures or military action. Through the centuries small gangs with deep political grievances, and usually with even deeper religious convictions, have always found ways instilling fear in the general population; and modern weaponry and communications make this much easier. Yet fear can be transcended by hope. Despite the potential power of terrorism, it has usually not been exercised, so that most societies at most times have lived in relative tranquility and security. This is because most societies at most times have found ways of addressing those grievances and undermining those convictions in sufficient measure that terrorist gangs never form – or, if they do, the flow of recruits dries to a trickle, and supporters are no longer willing to shelter the remaining members. Since modern terrorism is a global phenomenon, our hope must lie in global society doing the same.

The central value of the West, which it shares with, and to some degree inherited from, Islamic philosophy and law, is freedom – political and religious freedom. If we are to defeat terrorism, we must recognize that freedom is indivisible. Either everyone enjoys freedom, or ultimately no one can; either it is both political and religious, or it is neither. Thus we must strive for political and religious freedom across the entire world.

Political freedom means in the first place democracy and the rule of law; and insofar as predominantly Muslim countries lack these things, they are betraying the *sharia*, which, properly understood, guarantees them. This must then provide the framework for genuine economic freedom: not the false freedom that allows global corporations to turn poorer countries into virtual economic colonies; but the freedom that enables people to create businesses that can meet their compatriots' needs, and thence grow and employ others.

Religious freedom means in the first place mutual tolerance and protection for all faiths under the law; and insofar as predominantly Muslim countries lack these things, they are also betraying the *sharia*, which, properly understood, guarantees them. This must then provide the framework for genuine spiritual freedom: not the false freedom in which global sects strive for control over people's minds; but the freedom that enables people to find insight and inspiration from any and every source as it suits them.

The fruit of political and religious freedom is peace – at two levels. First, there is peace between peoples. When people enjoy both the prosperity that political freedom brings, and the contentment that religious freedom brings, mutual hostility becomes unthinkable. Secondly, there is peace between humanity and the planet itself. When people have control over their own economic welfare, they look after the environment on which it depends; and when they have control over their own spirits, they are happy with whatever their environment yields.

Fear of terrorism is horribly and painfully passive: there is almost nothing that most of us can do to protect ourselves. But the hope of freedom and peace can be active; every individual, family and neighborhood can contribute. We can begin to reduce our consumption of goods, especially primary products, from far-off lands, such as exotic fruits and flowers. If we work in large corporations, we can try to persuade them to disengage from activities in poorer countries. We can contribute to non-profit organizations that offer education in the West to people from poorer countries; and we can welcome such people into our homes. If we run businesses, we can try and hire immigrants from poorer countries. We can educate ourselves in the cultures and traditions of other countries and continents. We can withdraw from any involvement in doctrinal religious organizations, and participate in groups that practice religious openness. We can learn to be contented with what we already have, and then learn to be contented with a little less. And, of course, we can exercise our democratic rights in the direction of freedom. Thus we can all become foot soldiers in the *jihad* for peace.

A military and financial *jihad* against global terrorism, as America and her allies are waging, will take a very long time, as American leaders have warned; and although it may constrain terrorist activity, ultimately, as many western experts admit, it cannot be won. A *jihad* for peace, waged by striving for political and religious freedom across the world, will take an equally long time; but happily it can be won – and victory will render the first *jihad* unnecessary.